"Open your valise," the inspector said.

"Of course. Just let me find my key."

The inspector opened the suitcase, abruptly scooped up my clothes and pushed them to one side.

"Anything under here?"

"No. Nothing."

He glanced down at my trembling hands. "Uh, huh," he murmured. "Well, I think there is."

Angrily he gripped the edge of the fabric and ripped the bottom of the suitcase out, revealing the cardboard false bottom.

"Hashish!" he announced in a voice that echoed through the crowded terminal. Then he leaned toward me. "And you know very well this is hashish!"

Sunrise over Sanayeh

MARTI SINCLAIR
with
Marilyn Cram Donahue

LIVING BOOKS
Tyndale House
Publishers, Inc.
Wheaton, Illinois

First printing, Living Books edition, December 1983

Library of Congress Catalog Card Number 83-50416
ISBN 0-8423-6682-2
Copyright © 1983 by Marti Sinclair and
Marilyn Cram Donahue
All rights reserved
Printed in the United States of America

PRISON ARABIC PRONUNCIATION KEY

a'alama? (ahl-AL-muh)—why?

afu (AH-foo)—amnesty

aginabeya (ah-gun-ah-BEE-yuh)—foreigner

avouka (ah-VOO-kuh)—come on

ba'ad shwey (BA-ud shway)—I'll take care of you later

B'abda (BAHB-duh)—town outside Beirut where courthouse is located

Ba'labakk (BAWL-back)—mountain village

bukra (BOO-kruh)—tomorrow

fostu le juwa (FOH-stu luh JOO-wuh)—go inside

iftahi al-bab (if-TAH-hee al-BAHB)—unlock the door

infarad (IN-fuh-rad)—isolation room

istagal (ish-TAH-guhl)—work

kayfa halik? (KAY-fah hah-LIK)—how are you?

kefiya (kuh-FEE-yuh)—Palestinian headgear; this can be long enough to wrap around the body

kull-yaum (kool-YAHM)—every day

la (la)—no

loo (loo)—hole in the ground that served as a toilet

maa' fi my (ma fee MY-ee)—there is no water

ma fi shey (mah FEE shee)—nothing

memnua (mem-NU-uh)—forbidden

min fadlik (min FAHD-lik)—please

mudeera (moo-DEE-ruh)—female prison directess

n'am (nahm)—yes

ra'eb (rah-EEB)—male prison director

Ramadan (RAH-muh-dahn)—annual month of fasting

Ramal (RAH-muhl)—men's prison

Sanayeb (Sah-NAH-yuh)—women's prison

sharmoota (shar-MOO-tuh)—prostitute

shu bike? (SHU bih-kee)—what's wrong with you?

Sit (Sit)—title denoting married woman

tabbula (tah-BOO-lee)—Lebanese salad

ufatish (oo-FAH-tish)—search

yalla (YAH-luh)—hurry up

Yammoune (Yah-MOO-nee)—mountain village

zapher (SAH-feer)—a dark brown herb, commonly mixed with oil and spread on bread

CHAPTER

1

I sat alone, drinking Arabic coffee in a street café.

The sidewalk crowd jostled its way around me, clamorous voices mingling with Arabic music in a chaotic discord of sound. Horns blared and engines roared as cars wheeled out and tried to pass, slamming their brakes and narrowly missing horse carts, slow trucks, and each other.

It was only midmorning, but Beirut was already deep into the heat of a Mid-Eastern June, and I felt more and more uncomfortable in the black wool sweater and long skirt that I had chosen for the noon flight to London. My fur-trimmed coat lay over the back of a chair beside me. People were staring, and I didn't blame them. Only a fool would dress like this in the summer in Lebanon.

Never mind, I told myself. I wouldn't be here

much longer. I adjusted the high slit in the front of my skirt and tossed back my long hair. It fell nearly to my waist. I knew that its pale blondeness was a rarity in this part of the world. But I was too edgy this morning to enjoy the stares of the Arab men at the next table.

Dimitri loved when I wore my hair long and loose like this. But maybe I should have done something else with it today—tied it under a scarf, perhaps, or fastened it into a bun. I didn't want to be conspicuous. For once in my life, I didn't need to be looked at.

I sat there waiting until it was time. Then I paid for my coffee and started walking back toward the Alcazar Hotel. It seemed to me that Beirut was more nervous than usual this morning. But it was probably just the heat and the dust . . . and my own preoccupation with what lay ahead.

The yellow suitcase was exactly where I had left it in the lobby. I picked it up quickly, walked outside, and hailed one of the old-style Mercedes that served as taxis in Beirut. The driver put the suitcase into the trunk and slammed the door closed. I took a deep breath and forced myself to lean back against the seat.

Everything was going to be all right. Dimitri should have reached the airport by now. He would be watching, and waiting, and he had promised to take care of me in case anything went wrong. But it wouldn't. It couldn't. I could depend on Dimitri. I took another deep breath.

My driver swung into the heavy downtown

traffic, one hand twisting the wheel and the other pressing firmly against the horn. We made our way through the crowded streets of Zatuna, and then along the nightclub-famous Rue de Phenicie. A few moments later, I saw the tin-roofed hovels of a Palestinian refugee camp—low buildings crowded tightly together and packed with people. A donkey cart struggled along the road, and men with huge bundles trudged slowly through the dust, hardly seeming to move at all, as we sped past them.

Beyond the congested streets, sandstone houses clung silently to the sides of Lebanon's ancient hills, and fishing boats bobbed in Saint George's Bay. Mount Sannin rose steeply above the Mediterranean coastline, showing its snow-capped peaks. I closed my eyes and tried to remember the last ten days of pleasure and ignore the growing tightness in my stomach.

It was to have been a dream vacation. And in a way I guess it was. It had been exciting posing as the American wife of a tall, handsome Greek. We shared everything—Dimitri and I—our days and our nights. There were morning trips to the cool Jaita caves with their underground displays of stalagmites and stalactites; afternoons by the sparkling pool of the elegant Phoenicia Hotel; twilights on the balcony of our room as we sipped Campari and soda and watched the sun turn crimson and dip into the sea. Later, there was dancing in the moonlight—Dimitri's face against mine—Dimitri holding me in his arms.

We had lived the way I had always dreamed of living. And it had all been free—the gift of a man

9

called Leonidas—in exchange for one small favor.

The driver braked sharply, narrowly missing a startled pedestrian. I opened my eyes and held tightly to the seat. This was no time for dreaming.

Suddenly we were driving up the long boulevard that led to the terminal. I leaned forward and scanned the crowd for Dimitri's tall frame, trying to spot the dark brown pin-striped suit we had bought together in London.

He wasn't there—at least not where I could see him.

The cab pulled up in front of the terminal and stopped. The driver got out, unlocked the trunk, and put my yellow suitcase on the pavement. Then he came around and opened the door and waited for me to get out.

I hesitated. If only I could see Dimitri, I would feel a little braver. I scanned the area again. There were luggage men hovering around the loading zones and crowds of people milling and mingling. It was a disorganized, noisy scene, and I couldn't see Dimitri anywhere.

Suddenly one of the skycaps came over to the yellow suitcase, picked it up, and put it on a cart.

My mind seemed to be moving in slow motion while everything around me was on a fast track. I had to do something, so I got out of the cab, paid the impatient driver, and smoothed my clothes and hair. There was plenty of time, I told myself. I didn't have to hurry.

But my luggage was disappearing without me

through the double glass doors. So I did hurry—
right along through the doors, past a long line of
people and straight to the big square customs
table.

The whole airport was crowded and noisy
that morning, filled with families and Middle-
Eastern confusion. Little children pulled at their
parents and pushed at each other. No one was
paying any attention to me.

I looked at the customs inspector and felt one
brief moment of panic. If I wanted to back out,
this was my chance. There was no tag on that
suitcase. Nothing that would identify me at all.
I could walk away now and forget the whole
thing. But if I did, Dimitri would never forgive
me.

I watched the skycap lift my suitcase onto the
table and wheel his cart away. I saw the customs
inspector leisurely rummaging through a man's
suitcase. Finally he reached for mine.

He was a short stocky man with a big, full
stomach. He didn't look overly intelligent. His
hands fumbled as he worked, clumsy and slow.
It made me feel better just watching him. I felt
a surge of self-confidence. Hadn't Dimitri told
me it would be like this? I felt certain this fool-
ish-looking little man would pass me right on
through. If anything did go wrong, I knew what
to do. Dimitri had shown me how to use the
bribe money. After that, it was up to Dimitri. I
had to trust him. The rest of our lives depended
on my trust in him.

I stepped up to the customs table and stood
next to the yellow suitcase.

11

"Open your valise," the inspector said.

The expression on his face didn't change, but I saw something in his eyes . . . a flicker of expectation that said as clearly as words, "Here she is. This is the one."

For a second I couldn't move. *They know! Someone told them. They've been waiting for me.* Part of me raced ahead, panicked, looked for Dimitri, tried to turn and run. The other part held me there—smiled and nodded and said, "Of course. Just let me find my key."

I told myself that I was imagining things. He was just a stupid inspector. He didn't know a thing. *Be cool, Marti. Play it cool.*

But my hands were wet and shaking by the time I found the small luggage key, caught deep inside my wallet. "Sorry." I forced another bright smile. "I was afraid I'd lost it." I gave a tight little laugh, then reached over and tried to fit the tiny key into the lock. But my hands trembled and my fingers seemed numb. I kept missing the keyhole. Finally, I had to hold one hand with the other to steady it. The key slipped into the lock and the latches flipped apart.

The inspector opened the suitcase, and instead of feeling around in my clothes the way customs men usually do, he abruptly scooped them up and pushed them to one side. Then he began tapping on the bottom of the suitcase.

"Anything under here?"

"No. Nothing."

He glanced down at my trembling hands. "Uh, huh," he murmured. "Well, I think there is." His brown fingers began to tease the nylon surface, moving carefully back and forth. When he began pressing deep into the lining, I felt in my wallet and found the fifty Lebanese pounds that Dimitri had given me . . . just in case. I folded the bills into my palm and waited.

He was slowly wedging his fingers under the side band, pulling it up until the edge of the lining fabric was exposed and the black metal frame stuck out.

"What are you doing to my suitcase?" I tried to sound indignant.

He ignored my question and held out one hand to show me his fingertips. They were covered with a clear, sticky substance. "Can you tell me what this is?"

"I don't have any idea. Probably something from my cosmetics bag that leaked out."

He sniffed his fingers and shook his head. "It smells like glue to me."

I gave an elaborate shrug and slowly stretched out my arm toward him.

He reached out with one gnarled fist and gripped my wrist, turning my hand over and forcing it open. He gave a contemptuous snort and pushed the money aside. Angrily he gripped the edge of the fabric and ripped the bottom of the suitcase out, revealing the cardboard false bottom. Then he gave a quick jerk and the first slab of hashish lay exposed.

I was astounded. It had opened so easily—just like it was waiting to be opened. The glue hadn't even dried.

"What is that?" I demanded. "What is all that stuff? How did it get into my suitcase?"

13

He pierced the flimsy white cover material with his pen knife, and the brownish dust sifted out through the slit. "Hashish!" he announced in a voice that echoed through the crowded terminal. Then he leaned toward me. "And you know very well this is hashish!"

"I don't! I don't know anything about this. I don't know what it is, and I don't know how it got in my suitcase."

People were turning to look at us—to stare. I could see their mouths forming the word as it was repeated again and again—"hashish . . . hashish . . . hashish"—until the room was alive with the sound of it. Curious faces gathered around me, crowding closer and closer.

I felt my face tighten. I tried to swallow, but my mouth felt full of cotton, and I choked and began to cough instead. To my horror, I was beginning to tremble all over, uncontrollable quivers passing through my legs.

"Please," I protested. "I don't know what this is all about. I've never had any problems like this before."

The inspector looked at me and shook his head. "You'll have to come with me," he said. Then he picked up the suitcase and carried it, still open like an oversized book, in his arms.

Nobody made me follow him, but I did. I turned and followed him across the lobby, down a few stairs, and out a small side door into the hot Beirut sunshine.

CHAPTER

2

"Where are you taking me? What's happening?"
I asked the customs inspector again and again,
but he refused to answer. He looked straight
ahead and walked fast. I had to hurry to keep up.
I was almost running.

*Run, Marti. Run the other way. You're out-
side now—you can get away if you run.*

But I couldn't get away. Not in Beirut. Where
would I run to? To Dimitri? I didn't even know
where he was. So I followed the inspector along
the outside of the terminal building, in through a
side door, and down the hallway to a small office.

The door was open and I could see several
men standing around talking and looking as official as anyone ever does in Beirut. They all wore
the light green summer uniform of the Lebanese
Army, each with a Lebanese cedar tree on his
shoulder.

Their conversation died away as we entered, and they moved back, making an open pathway from the doorway to a desk on the other side of the room where a man in plain street clothes sat working. He looked up and said a few words in Arabic, and the inspector answered, then placed my suitcase on the desk. It was still open, showing my rumpled clothing and the exposed slab of hashish with the brown dust sifting out.

A babble of Arabic filled the room as the inspector gathered up my clothes in one bundle and tossed them onto a couch, then ripped out the other side of the suitcase to reveal another slab of hashish.

The man behind the desk motioned for me to come and sit in a chair beside him. He lit a cigarette and offered me one. Then he studied me slowly, taking in my clothes and the expensive tortoise-shell sunglasses that I held in one hand.

"What's your name, miss?" His voice was low and gentle, with only a slight accent. I thought he must be about thirty—only a few years older than myself. He was a nice-looking man, with warm dark eyes and wavy hair. He seemed cultured, and he was treating me with courtesy. It was more like a job interview than a police action. I felt myself relaxing a little. This man could see that I was no common criminal. He would question me, and then surely he would let me go.

"Marti," I replied. "Marti Sinclair." I smiled at him and tried hard to keep my voice low and steady.

"And this is your suitcase with the hashish in it?"

"Yes, it's my suitcase. But I don't know anything about any hashish. I've never even seen hashish before."

"Then how did it get in your suitcase?"

"Someone else must have put it there."

The look on his face told me it was an answer he had heard many times before. He leaned across the desk. "Of course someone put it there. But it is still your suitcase. You are going to have to do better than that."

I had underestimated him. He wouldn't settle for easy answers. I glanced out of the open window and saw a red and white plane marked with the tree of Lebanon. I had less than one hour to convince this man that I was innocent. But how? This was something I hadn't rehearsed. Dimitri had said not to worry. He would take care of any emergency. He would even take the blame. But he wasn't here to help me. I was playing this scene alone, and I couldn't sit here silently forever.

The customs official sighed impatiently and leaned back in his chair. "Look, Miss Sinclair, this is not a children's game we're playing. You have a suitcase full of hashish. That's called drug trafficking. In Lebanon it means three years in prison. Do you understand me? You could go to prison for three years."

I tried not to let my shock show. This couldn't be happening to me. Nice girls didn't go to prison.

I felt as if the room were getting smaller . . . smaller . . . closing in on me. There seemed to be no air at all coming in through the open window. A bubble of panic started somewhere deep inside me and rose until it threatened to burst in my throat. I wanted out of here right now!

The official lit another cigarette and leaned back in his chair. "I'm trying to help you, Marti. Now why don't you tell me where you got the hashish? Give me the names of everybody involved. If you cooperate, I might be able to let you go."

I glanced at the plane again. Could Dimitri already be on it? Would he leave without me? Oh, I didn't want to believe that. I needed to see him so badly—to talk to him—to have him make everything all right for me again.

Suddenly my mind clicked, and I remembered Alexandrou. Alexandrou Achilles—Dimitri's friend. He was as deeply involved in this as Dimitri was. I wasn't overly fond of Alexandrou, and it wouldn't bother me a bit to put the blame on him. Besides, I had no intention of sitting in a Lebanese jail while either Dimitri or Alexandrou went free. My mind began to form a plan—a way to find Dimitri—a possible way out for both of us. I wasn't going to be alone any longer.

I looked at the customs official, and I began to talk. "I'm not the only one who has had access to that suitcase."

He gave me a quick glance, then picked up his pen and began to write.

"I'm traveling with my fiancé. His name is

Dimitri Strongilis," I told him. I fished around in my purse and found the picture of Dimitri that I always carried in my wallet. "This is what he looks like. We're both booked on the noon plane to London. He should be checked in by now because he left ahead of me."

The official picked up the phone and called the luggage check-in. I heard him say Dimitri's name, followed by a string of Arabic. It sounded like he was giving instructions. He hung up and began interrogating me. "What are the two of you doing in Lebanon?"

I tried to make my voice pleasant, telling him that we were here on a holiday, recounting some of the things we had seen and done. I wanted him to think that—for me, at least—it had been only an innocent pleasure trip. I had to win this man over.

I didn't have to talk long. In ten minutes the door opened and Dimitri's brown suitcase was thrown on the couch.

"Is that his suitcase?"

"Yes, that's it."

Dimitri hadn't even bothered to lock it. Two of the men snapped it open and went through his clothes. Of course, there was nothing. There was no place to hide hashish in Dimitri's soft-sided luggage.

"It seems that your fiancé was careful not to get involved," said the official. "And now he has conveniently disappeared."

"He hasn't disappeared," I insisted. "I've told you that he's in the airport. I'm sure he's looking for me right now. He's probably frantic, wondering what's happened to me."

"For your sake, Miss Sinclair, I hope so. But the fact remains that we have to deal with the hashish in your suitcase. It didn't get there by itself."

"Of course not." I nodded, trying to sound agreeable. "When I told you that I wasn't the only one with access to my suitcase, I wasn't referring to Dimitri. He would never do anything to hurt me. I was thinking of this friend of his. Alexandrou Achilles. I . . . I don't want to get him into any trouble, but I'm beginning to think that he may be to blame for this whole thing."

The official picked up his pen again. "What about this Alexandrou?"

"Well . . . day before yesterday, he drove with us on an overnight sightseeing trip up into the mountains north of Beirut. My suitcase was in the trunk of the car, and it was never locked. Anyone could have opened it . . . someone obviously did. Alexandrou bragged about smoking hashish with some of the villagers in the mountains. He must have bought some for himself, then decided to use my suitcase to get it out of the country."

The official looked up from his writing. "Your fiancé could have done the same thing."

"But I told you. Dimitri would never do anything that would hurt me."

He nodded, but I couldn't tell what he was thinking. "And is Alexandrou also leaving for London on the noon plane?"

"No. I . . . I think he's staying in Lebanon a few days longer."

"Do you know the name of his hotel?"

"No, but it's right along the beach, near the Saint George's Hotel."

"Could you show me?"

I nodded, watching his face. Did he believe me? If he would only get busy and check on Alexandrou, he would find out about the money that Leonidas had wired him. I had no qualms about turning Alexandrou in. He was the perfect scapegoat. He even looked the part.

The official pushed back his chair and came around the desk to stand in front of me. "OK, Marti. If you really want to cooperate, there are two things you can do for us. First, you can walk around the airport with me and see if you can find Dimitri. We'll stop him if he tries to board the plane, but if he's still in the airport looking for you, you'll have to find him. Second, you can point out Alexandrou's hotel to me."

He held out his hand. "Before we leave, I'll need your passport and your airplane ticket."

I gave them to him and watched him thumb through the passport. "Martha Juna Sinclair. And you are an American?"

I nodded. Suddenly it became important for me to call him by name. I had to talk to someone who was more than a face. "Would you tell me your name?" I asked.

He looked up, a little startled. "My name is Nahzi," he said. Nahzi put my passport in the top drawer of the desk and my airplane ticket in his jacket pocket. Then he walked slowly to the doorway and stood, waiting for me to pass through.

It was then that I knew that I would never make that noon flight to London.

CHAPTER

3

Dimitri wasn't in the airport. The terminal building was fairly small, and I looked everywhere, with Nahzi walking beside me. I had been so sure I would see him. Where else could he be?

It was almost twelve-thirty before we were driving again, back through the pass toward Beirut on the same road I had traveled earlier. Only now I was sitting between two plainclothesmen in the backseat of an unmarked car. We drove through town, passing the Saint George's and then a long line of billboards. I leaned forward and told Nahzi to stop.

"There it is—that old hotel right along the beachfront."

We pulled over and got out of the car. My black sweater and long skirt were damp with sweat. And my long hair was wet at the roots. I was wearing new Italian shoes with four-inch heels, and I wanted desperately to take them off.

I followed the three men into the shabby hotel lobby where Nahzi showed the proprietor his badge and began to ask questions.

Nobody paid much attention to me, and I moved off a little to one side. Could I quietly back toward the door now, step outside, and disappear? I took one small step sideways . . . and stopped. It would be admitting guilt if I ran. And they would catch me, anyway. There was nowhere I could go for help in Beirut. I leaned wearily against the wall.

Oh, let them find Alexandrou. Then all this nightmare will be over.

"Yes," the proprietor was saying. "I remember Alexandrou Achilles. A young Greek with long bushy hair—you know, the hippy type. He was staying here, but he checked out yesterday. I don't know where he went."

We walked back out into the burning heat and sat in the car. I felt weak and sick and disappointed—and full of hate for Alexandrou. If he had only stayed put for another day, they would have had him—and maybe I could have gone free.

Nahzi looked back at me from the front seat. "How about it, Marti? Can you think of anywhere else he might be?"

I tried to concentrate. "We used to meet at the post office to make calls to London," I said. "Then Alexandrou would go with Dimitri and me to a little restaurant nearby. I can show you."

Nahzi drove quickly into downtown Beirut

and parked in the alley behind the restaurant. Inside, there were a few people eating, but no Alexandrou. My head was beginning to pound, and I felt a little dizzy. "Can't you do something else?" I begged.

Nahzi nodded. "We can eat lunch. I'm hungry." He led the way to a table, and the three men ordered. "You'd better eat something, Marti."

I shook my head. "No . . . I really don't want anything." I was afraid to eat—afraid it wouldn't stay down. I sat and watched them chewing and swallowing as if they had all the time in the world. But it was already two o'clock, and they still hadn't found Alexandrou. Or Dimitri. I put my elbows on the table and covered my face with my hands.

Nahzi finally sighed and pushed away his plate. "Wait here," he said, "while I make a call. Maybe something has happened back at the airport." The other two just kept on eating and eating. I looked the other way and swallowed hard, trying not to smell the food.

"Marti." It was Nahzi's voice. He had his hand on my shoulder. "Well, Marti, Dimitri must love you after all. He came back to the airport to find you . . . said he couldn't leave you in this predicament alone."

I caught my breath and fought to keep back sudden tears. Dimitri had come back! Now everything would be all right.

"He's waiting in the customs office," Nahzi told me. "But he gave my men the name of Alexandrou's new hotel, so we'll stop off there and pick Alexandrou up right now.''

We made our way back into Beirut's noisy stop-and-go traffic and drove to a part of town where I had never been. Old buildings with peeling plaster were stacked up together as if they were huddling for support. Wooden balconies hung precariously from rotting walls. Dark, open doorways led into darker halls, and tattered laundry flapped in open windows without glass. Garbage littered the sidewalks, and the narrow streets were crowded with milling people. I saw a few small boys running in the streets, dodging the honking cars. But mostly I noticed the women—tired looking and dirty, leaning in the shadows against crumbling walls.

Nahzi glanced at me in the rearview mirror. ''These are the kind of women who go to prison, Marti. Thieves and prostitutes. You wouldn't want to spend three years of your life living like them . . . would you?''

I didn't answer him, and in a moment he added, ''It's a good thing you are innocent—that you've told us the truth. Let's hope your friend Dimitri verifies all that you have said.''

Again, I didn't answer, and we drove in silence until we found Alexandrou's hotel, tucked back behind some of the old dilapidated buildings. The manager was still at lunch. There was nothing we could do but wait. I sank into a dingy, overstuffed chair in the lobby and closed my eyes against the filth and poverty.

When we find Alexandrou, it will all be over. They'll take him into custody and Dimitri and I will be free. Only a few more hours at the most.

Then this will only be a bad memory.

I said it to myself until I almost believed it. But something Nahzi had said in the car kept pricking at my mind. "Let's hope . . . Dimitri . . . verifies all that you have said."

Of course he would. Why wouldn't he? Suddenly my mind clicked. Dimitri didn't know what I had said. We had never planned on my having to say anything. *Oh, come on! Come on! Let's get back to the airport. I have to talk to Dimitri!*

But we didn't go back to the airport. We sat and waited in the hot little lobby until the manager finally came and took us upstairs and unlocked the door. Alexandrou's duffle bag was on the bed. The men dumped out its contents and began going through it. I heard them say they'd found his passport. But all I could look at was the leather coat that hung in the corner. *Dimitri's coat.* I had last seen it draped over his arm when he left me for the airport. Sometime this morning he had come here—to see Alexandrou. But when . . . and why?

Nahzi left one of his men at the hotel in case Alexandrou returned, and we began the drive back: through the congested area of downtown Beirut, past the Saint George's, up along the main street, winding along by the beach cafés, past the refugee camp, and then on toward the airport. My head was throbbing now, but so were my feet. I was aware of the terrible heat: my damp clothes clung to my skin; my hair lay wet and limp against my cheeks. But my thoughts were with Dimitri.

27

What was he telling them at the airport? Why had he gone to see Alexandrou? What would he say when he saw me? "Marti is innocent. She doesn't know a thing about any of this." Oh, how I willed him to say that.

I saw him in my mind: tall and dark—as handsome as a hero from Greek mythology. And he had such a way about him. He was a commanding person who made things happen, and he had promised to make things happen for me. I wanted to believe him. I had to believe him.

With a shock, I realized that my life was now in Dimitri's hands. Dimitri . . . Dimitri . . . I held his name in my mind like a lifeline. Dimitri would make everything all right.

He was sitting in a chair in the customs office. His shoulders, always so broad and straight, were slouched forward, and his dark hair hung in wet strands over his forehead. He looked tired and humiliated and defeated, and I felt humiliated for him. His pride and confidence were gone.

But I choked back the tears when I saw his hands—the hands that had held mine—that had loved me. They were shackled together at the wrists, and he had to raise them both to his face to smoke the cigarette that he was holding between his long, slender fingers.

"Oh, Dimitri," I wanted to cry. "What have they done to you?" But I didn't. The important thing now was to let him know what I had done—what I had said about Alexandrou and our trip to the mountains.

I walked directly across the room and stood in

front of him. "Blast that Alexandrou!" I exclaimed. "Look what a mess he's gotten us into. I hope they find him so we can get this cleared up."

He looked up at me, and I saw the surprise on his face. "Marti," he said softly, "I've already told them the truth. They said it would be better for you if I did." And then he looked away, as if he couldn't stand the shock on my face.

The truth? What did he mean by the truth? His words hit me like a fist in the stomach. They took my breath away. Had he told them the "truth" that I was innocent—or the truth that I was as guilty as he was?

I leaned over close to him. "Dimitri," I pleaded. When he finally looked at me, I whispered, "Dimitri . . . you promised!"

"That's enough!" Nahzi came across the room and stood between us. "I don't want you two talking together. On your feet, Dimitri. I'll speak to you in the next room." They went out together and I sat in Dimitri's seat, facing a uniformed officer behind the desk.

His eyes caught mine, and I tried to hide my confusion—my distress over not knowing what Dimitri had really told them. "Your fiancé did not speak well of you," he began. "Would you like to hear what he said?"

Yes . . . no . . . I didn't answer. I couldn't. But he told me, anyway—that Dimitri had told them that he was helping me carry the hashish for a London shipowner named Leonidas, so that we could have enough money to marry and go to America.

"That's not true!" I said. "He was never helping me carry hashish. I . . ." I stopped in time. I had almost blurted out that I was helping him. "I never knew anything about the hashish," I finished lamely.

"Is any part of his statement true?"

I hesitated. I never knew Dimitri wanted to go to America and get married. Maybe that part was true for him. I didn't know whether or not to deny it. In my confusion, I began to nod.

The officer held up his hand to stop me before I could begin to speak. "One minute, Miss Sinclair." He hesitated, then went on quickly. "I'm going to tell you something, and I hope you will listen. You will go to prison for sure if you try to protect this man. He has only been looking out for himself and you had better do the same. I advise you to say what is best for you and do what you can to get free. This Dimitri is not worth your trouble. You would do well to forget him."

He was leaning across the table tapping his pencil at me as he talked. He seemed so sincere. And yet, how could he know what Dimitri was really like? How could he understand our relationship? I couldn't believe that Dimitri had deliberately tried to incriminate me. He was confused and worried, and he had done what he thought was best for me. I had to trust him. I just had to. If I listened to this man, I would be betraying Dimitri.

I leaned forward. "Please let me see him. I know he will tell you I'm innocent—because it's the truth. I can't believe he said those other things. Just let me talk to him for a minute. Please!"

The officer looked at me for a long moment before he got up and led the way to the next room. Dimitri was sitting in a chair. He still wore his suit jacket in spite of the late afternoon heat, and beads of sweat stood out on his forehead. He seemed so tired, so limp all over.

I knelt down in front of him and put my hands on his knees. "Dimitri . . . please tell them . . . the real truth."

He looked at me, his eyes touching mine, and I felt him reach out to me, though he sat motionless in the chair. *The truth, Dimitri. The truth we agreed on. The truth you promised me.* I could see the anguish in his face and then a look of terrible regret.

He didn't take his eyes from mine. "She is innocent," he said. "She didn't know anything about the hashish. I put it in her suitcase myself."

One officer came forward. "That's not what you said a few minutes ago."

"I made a mistake," Dimitri answered. He was still looking at me. "Is a person allowed one mistake in his lifetime?"

I couldn't answer him, and I saw a terrible sadness in his eyes. "Marti . . . please . . . I would never hurt you. . . ." His voice broke. He tried to hold back the tears. But his face crumpled, and he began to sob, painfully, so that the other men looked away.

31

I ached for him—wanted to reach out to him, but the officer motioned me away. After a few minutes, Dimitri held up both arms, still held together at the wrists, and tried to wipe the tears away with the sleeve of his jacket.

"I'm telling you the truth," he told the officer, "so please write it down."

They made me leave him then. I went with the officer back to the other room and watched him record Dimitri's final statement, writing from right to left in the flowing, intricate Arabic manner.

Finally he turned the papers over. "I'm doing the best I possibly can for you, Miss Sinclair." He watched me for a moment. "Would you like something to eat—a sandwich or a cup of coffee?"

"No, nothing." I shook my head. "But I—I would like to change my clothes. I'm so hot and uncomfortable in these."

He nodded and pointed to a storage room. "You can change in there."

I went to the couch where my clothes still lay and pulled out a pair of lightweight summer trousers, a loose blue cotton blouse, and my most comfortable walking shoes.

The storage room was small and crowded with boxes, and there wasn't any fresh air. But it was such a relief to peel off my heavy clothes and let my skin breathe. I changed quickly, then went through my purse until I found a rumpled piece of paper with the name and address of the family we had contacted in the mountains when we went to buy the hashish. It could be incriminating, I thought, and I ripped it up into little pieces and stuffed them into one of the boxes stacked against the wall.

When I went back into the customs room, the officer gave me a huge paper sack—like a tall Salvation Army collection bag. "You can put all your things in this," he said. "Your suitcase has to be kept for evidence."

I wondered what they expected me to pack my things in when I caught the next plane out of here, but I was too tired to ask. I just sat down on the couch and did as I was told. Then I opened my leather bag and pulled my hair back off my face into a knot at the back of my neck. The cooler evening air came in through the open window, and I let it wash over me. But I couldn't relax. My stomach was in knots. Why was all this taking such a long time?

I leaned back and closed my eyes. But I felt so shaky inside. There was no way to rest. I could do nothing but wait.

Sometime, much later, I heard Alexandrou's voice in the hallway. "What do you think you're doing? I'm a Greek citizen. I want to call my embassy."

He lurched into the room, with two officers shoving him from behind. His long curly hair hung in thick wet loops, and he was wearing jeans and leather boots. His wrists were handcuffed together.

As soon as he saw me, he began to whine. "Why have you done this to me? What have I ever done to you?" His voice broke. He looked puzzled, hurt. I turned my face away. Alexandrou could rot for all I cared.

Suddenly the room was full of officers, and Nahzi was there, leading the questioning. "Tell us how you did this. Where did you get the hashish? How did you know where to go in the mountains?"

Alexandrou gasped as they shoved him onto the couch and pulled off his boots. The same officer who had searched my suitcase took them one at a time and inspected them thoroughly— the lining, the stitching, even the gravel caught in the edges of the soles.

Then they jerked him to his feet and frisked his clothing, taking away his wallet and cigarettes. All the time Alexandrou was loudly denying everything.

"I'm just a tourist," he insisted, "an artist passing through Beirut."

"There's nothing on you," Nahzi admitted, "but that doesn't prove a thing. This lady says you went with them to Yammoune."

"I didn't. I went to Ba'labakk with some friends. We stayed overnight, and I returned alone."

"You've never been to Yammoune?"

"I don't have to answer your questions. I want to see someone from my embassy."

Nahzi walked toward Alexandrou. "I'm tired of your stalling and know-nothing answers." He grabbed him by the shoulders, spun him around, and slapped him hard—once, and then again— across the face. "We have ways to make you talk," he said. "And I'm running out of patience." His voice was grim and threatening.

Alexandrou lifted his head, and I saw the angry red welts that were forming. He looked at me with such hatred. I was glad that I wasn't alone with him in the room.

"Tell me about Leonidas," persisted Nahzi. "What is your relationship with him? And why did he wire you money?"

"Leonidas is a family friend. My father and I own buildings in Athens. Sometimes we borrow money from Leonidas and return it gradually."

"And he sent some money to you here in Beirut?"

"That's right."

"What did you do with it?"

Alexandrou shrugged and looked at the floor.

Nahzi moved closer. "It would be wise to answer me," he said.

"I . . . I don't have it anymore. I lost it near the post office."

There was a short silence, and then the room was filled with laughter. Nahzi shook his head in disgust. Then he motioned to one of his men. "Go and get the other one."

"Do you know this man?" he asked Alexandrou, pointing to Dimitri.

Alexandrou nodded. "I met him in front of the Saint George's Hotel. We got together a few times after that, but there is no relationship between us."

"That's strange," Nahzi told him. "Dimitri says that he met you in London. That your friend Leonidas sent Dimitri and his fiancée to

Beirut to bring back hashish. They both swear that you went to the Yammoune village with them. Dimitri says that you and he got the hashish together. We have their sworn statements."

Alexandrou shook his head violently. "I deny everything." Then he began to whine again. "Why are you treating me like this? I'm innocent. I want to talk to my embassy."

Nahzi gave an exclamation of disgust. "Take them out of here," he ordered. I watched as Alexandrou and Dimitri were handcuffed together and led from the room. Dimitri didn't look at me. He didn't seem to be looking at anything.

I looked up at the clock on the wall. It was nine o'clock. "Where are you taking them?" I asked. But no one answered.

"You can sleep here for the night," Nahzi said. And he followed the others out into the hall.

I spread my coat out on the couch in the customs room and lay down there. The window was still open, and the breeze was cool. For a while I could hear voices. Then everything was quiet. Now and then an officer looked in, but nobody spoke to me.

I could see the moon shining in through the window, sending silver shafts of light across the floor. Out there was freedom. But not for me. There was no one in Lebanon who could help me if I escaped from this room.

I wished I had never come to Beirut. I wanted to go back in time and change it all. Back to the lobby and not have picked up the suitcase. Back to the village and not have gotten the hashish. Back to London . . . back to America. For the first time in a long time I wanted to go home.

But I couldn't. All my choices had led me to this little room where I lay now—tired and lonely and afraid. I closed my eyes. But I didn't sleep at all that night.

CHAPTER

4

"*Yalla! Yalla!*" The impatient officer kept urging me to hurry. He had come with me early in the morning from the customs office to the airport lobby where the long-distance calls were made. "I can't wait any longer," he insisted. "You must finish now."

It was six o'clock in the morning and I had not eaten for twenty-four hours. But I had managed to wash my face, touch up my makeup, and comb my hair. Now I had permission to make a telephone call, but I wasn't having any luck. It was Saturday evening in California, and everyone was out.

"Please," I begged the clerk. "Tell the New York operator to try those numbers again."

"You tell her," he said, and handed me the phone.

I took the receiver and clenched it tightly. "Listen to me, please. This is important. I must reach someone in the States." I gave the operator the numbers again: my mother's, my friend Marita's, and Larry's—the psychiatrist at the counseling center I directed.

She must have caught the urgency in my voice, for she promised to keep dialing. Through the heavy static, I listened to the sound of a phone ringing. I bit my lip hard. Please . . . oh, please. Someone answer!

There was a click—and I heard a voice at the other end. Marita's voice!

"I have a collect call from a Miss Marti Sinclair in Beirut, Lebanon. Will you accept the charges?"

"Yes . . . sure . . . what is it?"

"Listen, Marita. I'm at the Beirut airport, and I'm in trouble. Get a pencil and paper and write this down."

There was a pause. And then, "OK, Marti. Go ahead."

I took a deep breath and began. "Dimitri put hashish in my suitcase, and I've been picked up at customs. They're accusing me of trying to smuggle it out of Lebanon." I glanced behind me and saw the guard listening intently. I raised my voice so he could hear. "I didn't know it was there, Marita. I don't know how he did it. It's just awful. I could go to prison for three years."

"Oh, Marti, this is terrible. What can I do? Are you all right?"

"I'm OK right now, but things don't look too good. Now listen . . . I want you to call my mother and tell her what's happened. Then tell Larry and the board of directors at The Bridge . . .

but not the staff. They don't need to know."

"Yalla! Yalla!" the officer yelled. "You have talked long enough."

"Marita, I have to go. Please, please get somebody over here to help me out." I gave her the name and telephone number of a Lebanese lawyer the agent at the nearby ticket counter had suggested. I didn't know anything about him, but at least he was some sort of contact, a way my mother and friends could reach me. "Please, Marita," I said again. "Help me. I really need your help." My voice broke, and I had to hand the phone back to the clerk.

Almost immediately I felt a hand on my shoulder. The officer took me straight back to the customs room where Nahzi was waiting.

"Did you get your call through?"

I nodded. "Yes. I spoke to my friend. She's going to contact people who can help me."

"For your sake, I hope so. We're going to have to take you to Surete now—back into Beirut."

I got my brown paper bag with all my clothes in it, picked up my coat and purse, and put on my red straw hat that flopped down around my face. When I added the large tortoise-shell sunglasses, I felt camouflaged, and I managed to hold my head high as we left the airport.

Things were definitely looking better this morning, I told myself. I had talked to Marita— my very best friend. I could trust her to get things moving. I felt a little bad about lying to her about my innocence—but I would explain it all later, in a few days, when I was home again.

By eight o'clock in the morning we were in a part of Beirut I had never seen, riding in a government jeep up to an old brick building with big iron gates that opened to let us through. The courtyard was filled with unkempt, unshaven men who milled about aimlessly. I could feel their eyes upon me as soon as I got out of the jeep, watching me, following me, as I was led up the wide marble stairs and into the foyer.

It was a big room, imposing, with a high ceiling and stone floor. It looked very old, and it smelled musty. I was taken into an office where a man sat behind a desk with my file spread out before him. He looked up and peered at me over his glasses.

"It doesn't look good for you, miss. Your boyfriend says you knew about the hashish."

"I know he said that at first. But later he admitted that he had lied."

"It's too bad he said it at all."

I could hear Dimitri's voice in the next room—and then Alexandrou's. In a moment they appeared in the doorway, still handcuffed together. A guard motioned for the three of us to follow him down a hall and outside onto a veranda that overlooked the courtyard. He walked a little to one side and stayed there, watching us. Alexandrou stood motionless, stone-faced and angry. But Dimitri turned to me at once, concern showing in his eyes.

"Are you all right, Marti?"

I nodded. "I stayed all night in the customs room. Nobody bothered me."

"Marti, I want to explain—I only said you

knew because I thought it was best to tell the truth. It was a mistake—I made a terrible mistake. Don't be afraid, darling. I'm going to get you out of this."

He looked at me the way he used to, on the nights we had spent together. He always had a way of reaching out and touching me with his eyes. "You believe me, don't you?"

How could I not believe him? He made me feel so loved. I nodded my head.

"We'll get a good lawyer. I know how these countries work. If you get a good lawyer and you can pay, then you can get out. Stick with me, darling. I promise I'll take care of you. I'll make them believe you didn't know a thing."

I nodded again. I had been right to trust him. Dimitri would get me out of this mess. It would all be sorted out soon, and I would be free to go home.

We couldn't speak anymore, for another guard came and led us down the steps to where a car was waiting.

Forty-five minutes later we were standing high on a hill in the town of B'abda. Beirut lay nestled far below, its congested buildings crowding the harbor. But B'abda seemed to be in another world. The huge, old red-brick court-house building—the B'abda Palace—stood grim and foreboding before us.

One of the officers motioned for us to follow him through the entrance corridor, then immediately down a flight of steps to the left. The stairs were narrow and dark and precariously littered with bits of dirt and stone. I struggled with the big sack that contained my clothes and felt cautiously for each step, trying not to lose my balance.

We reached a landing, turned a corner, and began another descent. It was even darker here, and the walls were cold and wet. Suddenly a terrible stench rose up from below to meet us. I coughed and gagged and tried to breathe through my mouth. But the smell of old urine, excrement, and mildew was unavoidable. It seemed to come out of the walls of this place.

"Oh, Dimitri," I gasped. "This isn't a courthouse. It's a dungeon!"

We reached the bottom—the basement level, I supposed—and stood, blinking, trying to adjust our eyes to the darkness.

One bare electric bulb hung from the low ceiling, and in the dim light I could see three cagelike cells built underneath the staircase to my right. Down the hall straight ahead were others that seemed larger. They all had heavy iron bars and reminded me of animal enclosures in the zoo.

"You wait here," ordered one of the guards. He motioned for me to stand directly under the light. I rested my bag on the floor and watched while Dimitri and Alexandrou were led on down the dark corridor. I heard a key turn in a metal lock. Then an iron door opened, and slammed shut with a bang. My throat closed too—with a tight, choking feeling that made me want to gasp for air. Good clean air, from the daylight above. I wanted to break and run, to climb back up those littered steps. But I just stood there, peering helplessly after Dimitri into the darkness. What were they going to do with me now?

I felt a hand on my arm and was aware that a guard was steering me toward one of the smaller cells under the stairs. Each one of them was about three feet wide and extended into a darkness I had no intention of exploring. The ceilings sloped, so that the first cage was only about four feet high and the others were each just a little higher. The guard motioned for me to go into the third one, where I could just manage to stand without bumping my head.

It was so dark. I couldn't even see if there was anyone in there with me. So I stood close to the bars where a little of the dim light came through. I stayed that way until my legs were tired, then squatted down, trying not to touch the stone walls or floor.

Little by little, my eyes became accustomed to the darkness, and I could see the filth scattered about on the floor and the old stinking blankets piled farther back in the cell. The thought of sitting down anywhere repulsed me. But I was so tired . . . so very tired.

Finally I put my shoulder bag down flat on the floor and sat on it, drawing my knees up tight against my chest so that I could rest my head on them.

I looked at my watch. It was close to noon. Quickly, I wound it. Knowing what time it was seemed, at that moment, to be my only reasonable contact with the world outside.

I heard a rattling sound and looked up to see a

young Arab tapping at the bars. He couldn't speak a word of English, so he put his hands to his mouth as if he were drinking, then looked at me, both eyebrows raised questioningly.

"Yes." I nodded. "A drink. Yes . . . yes. . . ."

In a few moments he returned with a small plastic demitasse of thick Arabic coffee, strong and full of sugar, and a sandwich which he held furtively, as if he were trying to sneak it through the bars. I got up to take them from him, trying to smile pleasantly, nodding my thanks. But his body odor was overwhelming, momentarily blocking out the prison stench, and I had to turn my head away.

I sipped the coffee and kept it down, then tried to eat the sandwich. It was the usual—a flat bread rolled around a cheese and tomato filling. But after a few bites I began to gag. I sat down heavily on my makeshift seat and put my head back down on my knees. At first I took deep breaths to keep from vomiting. But the smell of filth was so strong that I only felt sicker. So I turned my face sideways and tried to concentrate on the graffiti that was scratched on the walls.

I must have closed my eyes and dozed off, for I was startled when I heard the key turn in the lock. I looked up to see a guard pulling open the door and a young woman about my age entering the cell. She was tall and thin, conservatively dressed in brown corduroy pants and a white blouse. She wore no makeup, but her skin had a natural, healthy look. Her chestnut hair was parted in the middle and fell loosely to her shoulders. Everything about her was neat and clean. Even her nails were manicured. She looked as out of place here as I felt.

"Hi," I ventured.

She gave a little nod. "Hi."

There was something about her. . . . I took a chance. "Are you an American?"

"Yes."

"Well, what are you doing here?"

"I'm waiting to be taken upstairs. My court trial starts in a few minutes."

She seemed a little distant—preoccupied. I thought she must be nervous—worried about her trial. I could tell she wanted to be quiet, but I couldn't seem to stop asking questions. She told me her name was Laurel, that she had been in Lebanon for five months, and that she had just come from the women's prison.

"What's it like there . . . at the prison?"

She looked around at the small filthy cell. "It's better than this. But it's not real good. Don't get your hopes up."

"I may not even have to go there," I told her. "I could be released today."

She gave me a quick look. "Don't get your hopes up about that, either."

A guard was unlocking the cell. Laurel turned to me. "When you come, you can ask for me," she said. And then she was gone.

Time passed slowly, minute stretching on to minute in painful monotony. I changed my position often, looked at my watch, rested my head on my knees, listened intently to the muted sounds around me, and changed my position again.

It was later in the afternoon when I heard the sound of high heels clicking against stone. A young woman started to walk by my cell, saw me crouching on the floor, and stopped. The surprise on her face was obvious.

She came closer and peered in at me. "Are you an American?"

"Yes."

"Does the embassy know you're here?"

"No, nobody knows I'm here."

She pulled out a notebook. "I'll contact them for you. What's your name?" She wrote it down. "Don't worry. I'm a reporter for the *Daily Star*. I'll let them know you're here."

She was gone almost before she had finished speaking. I listened to her high heels clicking up the stone stairs. And then it was quiet again.

It was sometime later that one of the night guards unlocked my cell and motioned for me to follow him. He led me into the corridor where Dimitri and Alexandrou had gone, stopping at the first cell and opening the door.

"You go in there," he ordered.

I walked in and watched him lock the door behind me, then began to inspect my new surroundings. This room was larger than the little cage I had spent the day in. Here I could stand up easily and walk around. An electric bulb dangled from the middle of the ceiling, illuminating the area. It was very bright and glaring, and there was no way to turn it off.

Opposite the door was a line of vertical bars that extended from floor to ceiling. Beyond the bars was an open space about three feet wide that stretched along the outside wall. High up on the wall I saw a small cracked window and people's feet walking by on the sidewalk outside. The space was an open garbage pit, full of decayed food, old paper, and debris. The floor of my cell was covered with debris, too. On impulse, I gathered it up in my bare hands and stuffed it through the bars.

Over in the corner was the *loo*, a hole in the ground that served as a toilet. The floor around it was slimy and covered with excrement, and the hole itself was full of filth. There was no way to flush it. Nearby was a stone sink filled with muck. I tried the faucet and got a spurt of cold running water.

In another corner I saw a pile of mahogany-colored blankets. I picked one up and dropped it quickly. It was wet and slick and covered with mildew. I was beginning to realize that I might spend the night here, but I couldn't stand the thought of lying on those blankets. If only they would let me have my bag, I could get a few things out of it and make some kind of bed on the damp floor.

When the next guard who spoke English came by, I called out to him, "Wait . . . I want to talk to you." He came closer, looking curious. "Please let me get some things out of my bag. It's right over there against the wall."

He shook his head and walked on down the corridor. When he returned, I stopped him again. "I only need a few things," I pleaded. "I need to make myself a bed."

"Impossible. You use those." He pointed to the filthy blankets in the cell.

"I can't . . . I can't." My voice began to tremble. "They're so dirty. They smell so bad. Please let me have my things. I'll only take a minute."

He looked at me. There was a puzzled expression on his face. Suddenly he seemed to relent. He muttered something to himself and opened the door, motioning for me to be quick.

I gathered as much as I could and went back into the cell where I began folding the dirty blankets into the shape of a mat. Then I covered them with my pink nylon housecoat, like a sheet. I wadded up some smaller things and wrapped them in a towel for a pillow. My gray pigskin coat would serve as a blanket on top. It wasn't much of a bed, but it was a place to lie down, and I wouldn't have to touch the floor.

I forced myself to walk around the cell and kick my legs as high as I could. I needed the exercise, for I was stiff and sore, and my legs felt as heavy as lead.

As the evening wore on, the guards came by less and less often. The night shift, I reasoned, must be poorly staffed. My mind began to work. Surely this cell couldn't be far from Dimitri's. If I called out, maybe he could hear me. I went to the door and pressed my face close against the bars.

"Dimitri . . ." I called softly. Then, a little louder, "Dimitri . . .?"

"Marti . . . is that really you?"

"Oh, Dimitri, I'm sick. I feel terrible."

"I know, darling . . . I know. I'm going crazy wondering how you are. Listen to me, Marti. It's going to be OK. Just hold on a little longer. I've gotten ahold of the name of a good lawyer who can get us out. He's a member of the cabinet—a big political man called Ma'louf. If we pay him, he'll do anything for us."

"But we don't have much money."

"We'll work it out, Marti. Just leave the worrying to me."

What else could I do? I had to leave it to Dimitri. He was the only person I could depend on. "How are you?" I called. "Are you and Alexandrou together?"

He gave a short, bitter laugh. "We're in here with about thirty others. There isn't any room to lie down—no blankets. We have been crouching up against the wall, trying to sleep. But it doesn't matter. I'll be all right, Marti, as long as you stick by me."

I felt ashamed for complaining. The love in his voice wrapped around me like a warm blanket. I could trust Dimitri. I knew it. Even more, I believed it.

Calling softly back and forth, we began to discuss and plan our case, thinking of what we would say when we appeared before the magistrate, making sure our stories would agree. We practiced the details over and over again. Dimitri would swear I was innocent. Then he would say that he and Alexandrou had bought the hashish for personal use—because he had found out that the sentence for possession was only one year.

One year, I thought. Dimitri would have to spend one year in a place like this. I closed my eyes and listened to his voice. Once I heard Alexandrou arguing loudly in Greek. He shouted at me once. "Don't believe Dimitri. Don't listen to a thing he says. He's going to put the blame on us, Marti."

His voice repulsed me, and I turned and went to lie down on my makeshift bed, pulling the pigskin coat close against the cold night air. The electric light was so bright—burning—like a torch forcing its way into my head. I pulled a scarf out of my wadded pillow and put it over my eyes. Finally, mercifully, I fell into a restless sleep.

CHAPTER

5

It was Sunday morning in B'abda. Sunday morning in prison. I lay on the floor on my improvised mat, unable to get up. I felt hot, then cold, and I was weak from lack of food.

Come on, get up. You've got to move around and exercise.

But I felt too sick to move. It was so much easier to lie there, with my eyes closed against the horror of where I was—to let my mind drift back into the safer past.

There had been a lot of other Sundays before this one. My mother's voice was always the first thing I had heard. "Wake up, Marti. You'll be late!"

We hurried and dressed, my sister Mary and I. Sunday was a family affair, an unshakable routine. We ate breakfast, then went to church together. In the afternoons, we had company, sometimes international students from the university where my dad was doing research in neuro-physiology. Mom would cook a huge dinner. Afterward we read aloud—usually favorite old stories from the Bible.

The one I liked best was the story of Queen Esther. I never tired of hearing about her. She was so beautiful and brave, and her king loved her. How I wished I could be like that. I would look in the mirror and try to see myself as someone special—without teeth that stuck out and a face with bumps. I dreamed of being beautiful and loved—and having a king of my own.

We were a busy family. There was church and school, and we always had a houseful of students from the university. Sometimes on Saturdays I went with my dad to the lab and watched him work. Other times I helped my mother at home. We never went to dances or movies or watched TV, because my dad wouldn't allow it. He wouldn't allow short skirts, either. "There are certain things," he told us, "that a Christian family just doesn't indulge in."

That's why I couldn't believe it when he decided to indulge in a divorce.

I was fifteen and in high school. My dad had finished his research project and had found a job in Massachusetts. "I'm going to go ahead and find a place to live," he said, "and you can follow later." He packed up all his things, then gathered us together in the living room to say good-bye.

"Lord, bless and keep us until we meet again."

Those were his words. Familiar and comforting. But we never did meet again as a family, and he knew we wouldn't. Because he wanted a divorce.

Later, he wrote to me from Massachusetts. Confusing letters, blaming my mother, begging me to understand.

"It's not true," my mother cried. "It's your father who doesn't understand. He wants too much, Marti. He asks more of me than I am able to give."

I believed one, and then the other. I was in the middle. Our family had seemed so happy, and now there was nothing but bitterness and loneliness . . . and fear.

Be careful, Marti, I told myself. Don't let it happen to you. If this is what a Christian marriage gets you, you don't need any part of it.

I finished high school and started college. My job as a receptionist in a law office didn't pay well, and one of my friends told me that I could make more money working as a cocktail waitress. "What do you have to lose, Marti? You need the bucks, don't you?"

I applied and got the job. On Friday and Saturday nights I earned fifty to sixty dollars in tips alone. It took all the money I could get together to pay my expenses and stay in college.

I didn't go to church anymore. I told myself I didn't have time, and I didn't need to feel guilty, either. Surely God could understand how busy I was.

Then I met Ivan. "All work and no play," he chided me. "You need someone to show you how to live." It was an innocent enough friendship in the beginning, but it didn't stay that way. I felt a little guilty at first. But I got over it. There couldn't be anything wrong with doing something that made me feel so happy.

Later, there were other men. Lots of them. I was popular in college, and I loved it. It was exciting to be admired and flattered. I knew my mother didn't approve of my life-style, but she just didn't understand.

"Marti," my mother said, "if you keep this up, you're going to get pregnant. Besides, the way you're living is wrong. Marital relationships were meant to go with marriage."

I smiled and kept my own counsel. There was the pill . . . and there was abortion. As far as morality went, I knew that answer, too. The Lord hadn't meant for people to go without natural relationships. Probably the Bible had made some kind of mistake. Maybe it hadn't been properly translated.

I liked being touched. I liked being loved by lots of people. What difference did it make, as long as no one was hurt? Look what a "lasting" relationship and a Christian marriage had gotten my mother. Loneliness!

Well, I told myself, I'm not going to be lonely. Not ever!

There were one night stands, and there were affairs that lasted a little longer. But only one of them left a warm spot in my heart. I called him G. He was so special—someone I could have been willing to stay with. We even celebrated our birthdays on the same day. But he didn't believe in commitments, not even short-term ones. It didn't work out, but I never forgot him.

The year before graduation I met Jim, a young socialist interested in labor management. "Move in with me, Marti," he said. "We're better together than apart." I did like being with him. He was someone I felt I could really relate to. So it wasn't long before we were sharing an apartment. It was what we called an open relationship, which meant we could have as many friends on the side as we wanted. And I did. I felt no guilt. Why should I? The old morality was fine for others, but I didn't need rules and regulations to tell me what to do.

After graduation, Jim worked for the city as a labor consultant, and I began working as an intern teacher in a high school. Art was my love, but English was the only position open, so I took it.

I wasn't much older than my students, and they started coming to me with their problems. Before long, I was spending most of my free time with them. One student was into heroin. "Smoke marijuana," I advised, "but stay away from the hard stuff. And don't ever push it, or you'll get caught."

After a while I started an activities program—the kind of thing that you slip into without realizing that it is going to become an important part of your life. In the beginning, my idea was simply to work with Chicano kids after school. We had speakers, went on field trips, and generally just kept busy and off the streets.

But one day, the Santa Clara Mental Health Department contacted me and said there was money available for just what I was trying to do. They wanted me to write a proposal for a full-fledged organization. I was a little scared because I had never done anything like that before. But Jim encouraged me, and lots of people were willing to help.

Suddenly the money was granted . . . and there I was. I had to hire a staff, get a secretary, find counselors and social workers, and get men in the community to serve on the board of directors.

I had started with nothing but enthusiasm. But referrals came quickly from the police department and the schools. Before long, our clinic was a real counseling center. We called it The Bridge.

It was a success, but it didn't leave much time for Jim. Once he complained, "If I became a heroin addict, maybe then you would spend a little time with me."

It was the beginning of the end of a three-year relationship, and in a way it was a big relief. I had been thinking about G again, and Jim didn't really have anything more to offer me.

I called G. He always seemed to be there when I wanted him. We saw each other again, kind of off and on. But G still didn't believe in any kind of commitment. He never told me he loved me, and I really never knew how he felt for sure. I was nervous and tense and tired from work. When I came home every day, I did yoga exercises to help me relax. But the tension with Jim was growing. Finally, it reached the breaking point.

I made plans to go to Europe for my vacation, and he had a fit. "Wait until I can go with you," he said.

"No way, Jim. It's my vacation, and I'm taking it now. Anyway, I'm going with Sheila. We've planned this trip together."

I was tired and felt I had earned a vacation, so I was taking a whole month—thirty days—and Jim hated the whole thing. We argued constantly, about everything—even God.

"Well, if you believe in God," Jim would say, "what can he do? What are his powers . . . and his limitations? Who is he, anyway?"

"I don't know, Jim. I don't know the answers to any of your questions. I am just sure that there is a God somewhere. I believe in him."

"I don't understand how you can be so naive. It's your background. I guess they brainwashed you." Then he would say, "Marti, the proof is in the believer . . . so prove it to me."

And I would start to cry. "I can't, Jim. I just can't prove it, because I don't know how."

"OK, Marti. OK. You don't have to prove anything to me. Go ahead and believe in anything you want to . . . just don't spread it around, huh?"

Jim and I separated, and I was alone. I called G one last time, and he promised to come. We made arrangements—real plans to be together. This time, I told myself, it was finally going to work out the way I wanted it to.

But G never came. He got lost, he said. He couldn't find my place. I tried not to think about him anymore. For the first time in years, I was on my own.

And I was tired. My work at The Bridge had become overwhelming: clinical work, administration, counseling—I was beginning to feel as if I was in over my head. When my friend Sheila and I packed our bags and got on a plane in the spring of 1974, I felt as if I was ending more than one chapter in my life.

We began in London, then traveled to southern France by train. We wanted to spend Easter in Rome, but couldn't get hotel rooms because of the crowds. So we flew to Athens instead.

Wherever we went, we tried to meet people who would take us places . . . show us around. Sheila and I went our separate ways, but we always got together later to talk about what we had done. And we always did our traveling together.

One afternoon, Sheila and I were walking past Constitution Square on our way to the Sheraton Hotel, where we planned to sit in the lounge, have a drink, and meet someone interesting who would take us to dinner and a night on the town. Entertainment was all we had in mind. Greek men were too short to interest us.

But there was one Greek in Athens who was tall and lean, with big almond eyes—dark eyes—deep-set as those in Greek statues. He was really handsome in his tight-fitting Italian-cut shirt and smooth trousers. There was definitely something about him. . . .

He fell into step beside me and began to talk.

His accent was thick, but I found it charming. "You look like a dancer," he said. And then he smiled. "Perhaps it is because you are so tall . . . and graceful."

I was glad I had gone to the hairdresser that morning. My hair hung in deep waves around my shoulders, and I knew that it was shining in the sun. I was wearing sleek black pants, and a green blouse that I'd bought the day before. I felt on top of the world.

"No." I smiled back. "I'm not a dancer. But I do enjoy dancing."

He nodded. "I could tell. It's my job to look for good dancers. My business is to arrange shows for nightclubs all over Athens and Europe. I'm always on the lookout for new talent."

This sounded interesting. "I'd love to hear more about your job," I told him.

"Are you busy now?"

"My friend and I are on our way to the Sheraton . . . but we're not in a real hurry." I glanced at Sheila and gave her a knowing wink.

"Then why don't we stop right here? I'd like to buy you both a cup of coffee."

He pointed to a nearby sidewalk café. As we walked there, he stopped at a flower vender and bought two long-stemmed red roses—one for Sheila and one for me. We sat around a small table under a bright umbrella and sipped our coffee. Our conversation was light and meaningless, but Dimitri never took his eyes from my face. When we rose to leave, he reached out and took my arm.

"Will you come with me tonight?" he asked.

60

"I will show you something special."

I nodded wordlessly. I knew that something important was about to begin.

That evening he took me to a hill above Athens. We watched the worshipers from the little church on the hilltop carry burning candles from the sanctuary out into the darkness and begin the long walk down stepping-stone paths into the city, where they would separate and return to their homes.

The tiny flickering lights fanned out in front of us in all directions, until the landscape looked like a galaxy of twinkling stars. We stood without speaking. There was a peacefulness—a serenity in the air. I felt the evening breeze brush across my face. And then everything was still. I waited, almost breathlessly. It was like a lull in time—a moment of hesitation. I didn't turn my face to look at Dimitri, but I could feel him moving beside me. Then I felt his strong arm around my shoulders, pulling gently, coaxing me toward him. He reached out with his free hand and took one of mine. He held it carefully, as if it were a fragile thing, then quickly bent his head and gently kissed my palm. I looked up at him then, into his dark deep-set eyes, before I sighed and rested my head against his chest.

We stayed on the hilltop until all the flickering candles were far away, and we were alone with the stars.

Finally Dimitri smiled at me and said, "We haven't eaten, you know. Are you starving?"

I laughed. I hadn't even thought about dinner. The restaurants in Athens were closed because of the Easter holidays, so Dimitri took me to his home. His family lived upstairs in the family house, and he and his brother, Janis, shared the apartment downstairs. But his brother was away, and Dimitri and I were alone. We ate a light supper, then sat and talked until it was very late. It had been a long day, and I was getting tired. I stood to leave.

Dimitri put his arms around me. "Don't go, Marti. Stay here with me." He cupped my face in his hands and kissed me lightly on one cheek and then the other. "I'm afraid to let you out of my sight," he whispered. "I don't want to lose you, my darling." I closed my eyes. I felt his lips on mine, his arms gathering me close. Somewhere, far away, I heard a clock strike. But I didn't pay any attention to the time. I knew Sheila would understand.

I stayed with Dimitri for two weeks, spending my mornings at the museums and galleries while he was busy elsewhere. At noon every day we would meet at Constitution Square and plan the rest of our time together.

There were long drives out into the countryside, through little villages where we stopped and ate wonderful Greek salads, crusty bread, and hot roast lamb. Sometimes we ate at little family restaurants in the city or went dancing with Dimitri's friends. Then he would hold me close, with both arms around me, and I hardly heard the music.

Dimitri was the most exciting man I had ever known—suave, charming, and he had a commanding way about him. He made me feel protected and cared for. He seemed to know me so well, to understand me completely. When we talked together, he made my heart sing. With him, I could give up responsibility. I was free.

And I was as good for him as he was for me. "Marti," his mother told me, "you bring out the best in my son. You can even calm that terrible Greek temper of his."

Oh, what a temper Dimitri did have! But it was never directed at me. With me he was gentle, loving, understanding. He knew how much closeness I needed and how much space I required.

But time was passing, and my vacation was almost over. I had to be in San Francisco the first week in May to attend a meeting that was to determine whether the counseling center would get a grant to start a new pilot program. I had planned to fly to London first and spend a few days there. I wasn't really surprised when Dimitri said he was coming with me.

"We'll get a little flat," he said, "and I'll wait there until you come back to me." He reached out and pulled me into his arms and held me tight. "Promise me, Marti. Promise you will come back to me. Oh, what a life we can have together! We can travel in Europe, and live in London. But we will return to Greece every summer to visit the islands. Listen, my love, you can paint and draw again. Why did you ever stop? You can learn French. You can dance."

I put my arms around him and held him close. It was hard to believe that he was real, and that he was mine.

We went to London together and found a little apartment where Dimitri would stay until I returned. I wrote my mother and told her I was coming home, but only to find someone to take my place at work and attend my friend Marita's wedding. "I will be returning to London the first week of June," I told her, "to be with Dimitri Strongilis, a thirty-year-old Greek from a very good family. He works in theater and dance in London and Paris. He will help me find work."

I was walking on air—so sure of myself. And so sure of Dimitri. He loved me . . . wanted me with him forever. At last I had found what I had always wanted. Dimitri was all I needed to make my life complete. Even while I was sitting on the plane on my way home, I felt him close to me. I could close my eyes and hear his voice.

I listened. Someone was calling to me, but it wasn't Dimitri. I opened my eyes. I wasn't in an airplane flying to San Francisco, but on the floor of a dismal cell at B'abda, deep underground, beneath the light of day.

I focused first on the bars in front of me, then on the face of the same young Arab who had brought me coffee and a sandwich the day before. Slowly, painfully, I lifted my head, then tried to sit up.

He took some red cherries and another sandwich from the tray he was carrying and offered them to me through the bars. I stood up dizzily and made my way to the door. He looked at me closely and shook his head sadly, giving me a pretty good idea of what I must look like. I thanked him and made my way back to the bed. I ate a few bites of the sandwich, and then some cherries, chewing slowly, hoping the food would stay down. Then I lay back down, waiting for the dizziness and the sudden pain in my stomach to stop.

I swallowed again and again, taking deep breaths, but the nausea became uncontrollable. I crawled to the dark hole in the ground and vomited, trying to ignore the foul smell and the excrement that already filled it. Then I turned to the sink. It was slimy inside and filled with muck, but cool water came out of my faucet. I cupped my hands and splashed some on my face.

Then I straightened up and began walking back to my bed. My head was pounding, and little black flecks seemed to fill the air around me. I staggered and hit the wall, then collapsed on the mat. I closed my eyes and knew very little for the rest of that day and most of the next.

CHAPTER

6

My mind wandered in and out of crazy dreams. Once I woke and heard Dimitri calling to me from his cell. "Marti . . . Marti. . . ."

But I didn't answer him. I didn't feel like talking at all. I knew that it was sometime on Monday, and that I had developed severe diarrhea in the night. I knew that I felt very sick and probably had a fever. Sometimes the thought would come to me that I was going to die in this place. They would take Dimitri away to prison and leave me here, and no one would ever know what had become of me.

"Marti . . . Marti. . . ."

I wanted rest. I needed to go to sleep. But his voice kept coming. It sounded hollow and far away, like a long-distance telephone call.

"It's a long-distance call for you, Marti."

I was at home in San Francisco, and my mother was handing me the phone.

I took it and held it to my ear. "Marti . . . Marti. . . ." It was Dimitri's voice.

"Yes. Hello, Dimitri. It's Marti. I'm here."

"Marti, I miss you. When are you coming back?" His calls were regular occurrences at our house. Reassuring, loving calls that made me wish I were with him.

"I'm just finishing up last-minute details, Dimitri. It won't be long now." I hesitated, hating to bring up what was bothering me. "Dimitri, the money for my ticket hasn't arrived. Have you sent it yet?"

"That's one of the reasons I'm calling tonight. Listen, darling, I've had some bad luck at the tables. I lost a great deal gambling last week. There isn't any problem, of course, but it will take a few days to transfer funds from Greece and straighten it out. Can you handle the ticket, Marti? I promise I'll make it up to you."

"Well, I suppose so. Of course I can, but. . . ."

"Darling, you don't know how I want you to be here with me. Just come to me, Marti. Everything will be all right when we are together again."

"Dimitri. . . ."

"Listen to me . . . you are my love—my life. I can't live any longer without you."

The ticket didn't seem important anymore. I could almost feel his arms around me. I replaced the receiver and stood, smiling. What a fool I had been to have any doubts.

After I had returned to San Francisco, I had had a few second thoughts. After all, I did have a certain amount of security with my job at The

Bridge. I was respected there. And, I told myself, I had friends and family in San Francisco. If I returned to London, I would be taking up a new way of life, and that involved a risk.

Well, what of it? Nothing in my life so far had brought fulfillment. Finding what I was looking for was worth a risk. Nothing was really holding me in the States. Only pressures from work and broken relationships. Besides, I had already told all my friends about Dimitri—how he came from a wealthy family and had promised me the world.

I arranged for a six-week leave of absence from The Bridge. If things worked out with Dimitri, I would have plenty of time to tell them that I wouldn't be back at all. Then I packed my bags, brushed aside any forebodings, and boarded the plane with five dollars in my purse and a heart full of dreams and expectations.

But I had forgotten that you must have two hundred dollars to enter a country, or you can be considered a vagrant. Dimitri met me at the airport and had to vouch for me at customs.

"Marti," he laughed, "why did you travel with only five dollars in your purse?"

I put my arms around him. "Because it was all I had left. I had bills to pay, and I had to buy my ticket, and. . . ." Was it my imagination, or did I feel him stiffen? "Dimitri, did you expect me to bring a lot of money or something?"

"Of course not, sweetheart. You know your money doesn't matter to me. I am just surprised. Marti, it's not a good idea to travel with so little.

What if you had had an emergency?"

It was typical of Dimitri to worry about me. I felt reassured and loved. We went home to the little apartment where Dimitri had been waiting. He would take care of me now. My new life had begun.

For a while things were fine. The rent was paid, and Dimitri bought groceries so that I could cook intimate candlelight dinners for the two of us. Sometimes we visited friends, and in the evenings Dimitri would take me to watch him gamble. Sometimes he won, but more often he lost.

One day we went shopping in the stores along King's Road. "We'll use your Master Charge," he said. "It's simpler that way, and I'll pay you back."

"Why not use cash? It's even simpler."

Dimitri suddenly looked angry. "Because I don't have any cash. I lost it gambling. I'll get some more, but I have to wire to Greece, and that takes time. Now give me the Master Charge."

It was after that that he began borrowing from Leonidas, his shipowner friend. He used the money he borrowed to gamble some more and try to win back what he had lost. I watched him one night as he sat in the casino. My hands were sweaty, and I was so nervous he sent me away from the table.

"It's your fault that I'm losing!" he snapped.

When we got home, he apologized, taking me into his arms. "I don't know what made me act like that. I'm sorry, Marti. It's just that I want you to have things—I want to take care of you. I don't want you to worry.''

I looked up at him. "But you really don't have any money coming from Greece, do you?''

He didn't answer me. He didn't have to.

The next night he told me about some of his friends who had just come back from Beirut with hashish which they sold to their friends at a big profit. Leonidas was interested. He wanted Dimitri to go and get some hashish for him, and he promised to buy all that was brought back.

"I've decided to do it,'' he told me. "Alexandrou and I are going together, but we're going to Turkey instead.''

I was appalled. "It's too dangerous, Dimitri. What if something happens to you?''

He put his fingers against my lips. "You're not to worry. It's all right. I just want you to trust me. And, Marti, if you run short of money and need anything while I'm gone, you are to call Leonidas. He'll give you whatever you need.''

I did call him, and he met me for coffee and gave me twenty pounds. He didn't talk much, but I had the feeling he was watching me, sizing me up. For what?

I spent my days reading, writing, reflecting— and doing a lot of thinking. But most of all I missed Dimitri. When I finally got the telegram telling me to meet him at Heathrow Airport, I was happy and excited.

He walked through customs without a snag, but it wouldn't have mattered if they had searched him, because he had come back empty-handed.

"The hash wasn't any good," he told me. "Alexandrou and I junked it before we got on the plane." He sighed and put his arm around me. I could hear the disappointment in his voice. "A whole trip for nothing."

A few days later he went to talk to Leonidas. When he came home, he was smiling. "You really impressed Leonidas," he said. "He liked you so much that he's making us an offer."

I remembered the way the man had looked at me, sizing me up, almost as if he were putting me through some kind of test. "What sort of an offer?"

"He's willing to pay for us to vacation in Lebanon if you will agree to bring back the hashish in your suitcase."

I looked up at him, shocked. "*My* suitcase? Why do I have to carry the stuff?"

Dimitri's voice was calm, reassuring. "Because customs rarely looks in women's suitcases, especially American women's. I know couples who do this all the time, Marti. It works out better this way."

"But what if something goes wrong?" I asked. "What if they open my suitcase and find hashish in it?"

He laughed softly, as if I were a foolish child. "My sweet love, you know I would never let anything happen to you. I would take the blame and tell them that you didn't know anything about it. But it won't happen that way. Hashish is smuggled out of the country every day. It's a big business in Lebanon. Friends of ours just got back last week, and nothing happened to them. Listen, they have a special family they always go to. Our friends know them—they do a good job, and they can be trusted."

"Oh, Dimitri . . . I don't know." I was honestly nervous. The whole idea frightened me.

"You would not want to miss Beirut, Marti. They call it the Switzerland of the Middle East, and it's full of the kinds of things you enjoy."

I wanted to please Dimitri, and I knew he wanted me to say yes. "Give me a little while to think about it," I pleaded. "I just need to get used to the idea."

The next night we went to the apartment of some Greek friends. They had hashish, and Dimitri showed me how to smoke it. I had had marijuana before, but it was nothing like this. One little puff, and my head began to spin, to whirl. I felt disoriented, confused, unsure of what I was doing. I began to cough and couldn't stop for a long time.

"It's good stuff," Dimitri explained. "This hashish came from the village you and I will go to."

His friends nodded. "We brought it out without any trouble at all. They didn't even open our suitcases."

After that evening, Dimitri began arranging our trip, and I went along with his plans. I was still nervous about the possibility of being caught, but it didn't really seem very likely. And I did want to travel and see new places. Beirut sounded fascinating. By the time we were ready to leave, I was excited at the prospect of a vacation on the Mediterranean.

For almost two weeks we lived in luxury in Beirut, enjoying the sights by day and nightlife under the stars. I tried not to think of why we had really come.

But the day finally arrived, and I couldn't put it out of my mind any longer. We rented a car and got ready for the trip into the mountains of northern Lebanon, to the village of Yammoune. Alexandrou Achilles was going with us, and he and Dimitri were to make the deal together.

We started early in the morning, because it was a long, four-hour drive. Soon we left the city far behind. The pavement ended, and we were on winding dirt roads that twisted deep into the mountains. It was such beautiful country—I began to relax and enjoy the scenery.

After a while, we began to see field after field of green hemp growing in cultivated rows like tall young corn. The air was thick with the smell of it. It was all around us—everywhere. I knew that in this part of the world the dried leaves and stalks would become hashish—literally a dried herb, but actually the powerful narcotic that I had sampled in London a few weeks before.

It seemed so natural to see it growing like this in well-tended farmlands. Hashish is common here, I told myself. It was obviously an acceptable thing. I relaxed a little more, and some of my fear began to seep away.

We had a map to help us find the village, but it didn't seem to help. Over and over again we had to stop along the road and ask the question, "Yammoune? Where is Yammoune?"

By the time we finally found our way there, it was high noon, and we were hot and tired. Alexandrou was beginning to get on my nerves. I didn't like him, and I didn't trust him. There was a nervy brashness about him that was insincere, and he was boastful and arrogant. I wondered how Dimitri could call him his friend.

I was under the impression that the family we were looking for lived right there in the village, that Dimitri knew them well, and that the deal was all prearranged.

But Dimitri had no idea where they lived, only their name. We parked the car and got out to look around. White stucco houses nestled against the mountains, seeming to cling precariously to the slopes, and the few winding dirt roads that led out of the village were unmarked.

Dimitri stopped a couple of teenage boys and asked them if they knew the family. They grinned and nodded. "We show you." They got into the car and directed us onto one of the dirt roads out of town and along the edge of a small lake. Finally, they motioned for us to stop and pointed up to a little whitewashed stone house that could be reached by climbing up an embankment faced with flat sheets of rock that were hewn into crude steps.

It looked deserted, but inside were two small sleeping rooms with mats on the floor and several young men smoking hashish. I glanced at Dimitri. "This doesn't look like the family house," I said.

One of the young men seemed to understand. He stood up and walked over to us. "Family?" he queried, and then, "I take you there."

Alexandrou's eyes had begun to gleam when we walked through the door. I could see him sniffing the air eagerly, like an animal looking for food. "I think I'll stay here," he told Dimitri. "You can go ahead and make the deal without me."

I was happy to leave him there. I hoped he would decide to stay with them permanently. But Dimitri wasn't pleased. "You always want the easy way out," he said. "You expect me to do your dirty work for you."

Alexandrou shrugged and sat down on one of the mats. I touched Dimitri's arm. "You don't need him," I said. "You'll be better off without him." I wanted to get on with it and get out of here, and I didn't want Dimitri to start losing his temper now. We climbed into the car together and followed the young man's directions along another dirt road that wound through the hills.

When we arrived at the family home, a young Arab girl about ten years old answered our knock. She invited us into a large living room lined with furniture—some chairs, a table, a sofa, then a few more chairs—like the reception room of a doctor's office.

Almost immediately, an old woman entered and served us a red drink that was very sweet and tasted like rose water. This whole thing was beginning to seem like a family affair. What could be so wrong about something that included grandmothers and small children?

We were just beginning to sip our drinks when Alexandrou slipped into the room, followed by a young continental-looking man. He was tall and dressed in European fashion, with his tight-fitting shirt opened casually in front to expose his chest. He greeted Dimitri in strongly accented English, introducing himself as Shariff. Whenever he couldn't express himself, he switched to French, which Dimitri spoke fluently.

After a few moments of conversation, Shariff brought out a metal tray with lots of round balls of different grades of compressed hashish. They looked like little clods of dirt and were the rusty color of rich soil. Dimitri took a little of each mound into his palm, spread it out with his fingers, and smelled it.

"Want to try some?" Shariff offered.

"No, thanks. I don't smoke." Dimitri had told me before that a buyer who knows what he is doing never smokes in front of the seller. You should be able to tell good quality by the smell and feel.

But Alexandrou had different ideas. "I'd like to try some," he said. Shariff gave a little smile that made me know that Dimitri was right. But he mixed some of the hashish with tobacco and gave Alexandrou a cigarette.

Dimitri tapped one of the balls of hashish on the tray. "How much?" he asked.

"One hundred dollars per kilo."

Dimitri nodded. "We want four."

My yellow suitcase was brought into the

house, and then Shariff led us up a flight of steps, through the kitchen, and into a small room that was bare except for a few mats that lay against the far wall.

My suitcase was laid open in the middle of the floor, and my clothes were taken out and put aside. Then the hashish was brought in like a pile of rich brown soil and heaped on a big sheet. Four kilos looked like a staggering amount when it was all loosely heaped together like that. I couldn't see how they expected to get it all into my suitcase and put my clothes back in, too.

But the old grandmother was already measuring the bottom of the suitcase with a piece of string. Then she left the room, and Shariff started the slow, careful process of tearing away the lining. In a little while the grandmother returned with two thin pouches that looked like open pillowcases and were the exact size of the suitcase top and bottom. Shariff and the other young men began stuffing the hashish into these bags. As they picked it up in their hands, a fine dust drifted through the room, permeating the air. The sweet, pungent smell was so strong it made me feel woozy.

I left the room, feeling like I was staggering, and went back through the kitchen to steps that led to a flat, rooftop terrace at the top of the house.

I sat for a while on the little wall that circled the rooftop and looked out over the countryside. The sun was going down behind the hills of Lebanon, and a dark shadow fell across the miles of hemp fields, waving gently in the evening

77

breeze. There was a sudden chill in the air. I shivered and rose to go back inside.

When I returned to the bedroom, all the hashish had been ironed flat inside the thin cloth pouches, and the open sides had been sewn shut. They resembled two stiff sheets, each about one quarter of an inch thick.

I watched them place the sheets into my suitcase, replace the cardboard over them, and then glue back the silk lining over the top. Little chips of charcoal were stuck around the sides of the suitcase to camouflage the odor, and a touch of perfume was added to help cover the smell.

Shariff approached Dimitri. "For a little more money, we will pay off the customs officials for you. Then you will surely pass through without a problem."

Dimitri hesitated, then shook his head. "It's not necessary," he said. "We don't expect any problems."

Shariff shrugged. "Then we hope God will be with you."

By then it was past midnight—much too late, they told us, to return to Beirut over those winding mountain roads. We had no choice but to stay the night with the family and drive back early the next morning.

They brought us scrambled eggs with sugar and mountain wheat bread, a round flatbread as thin as paper and about sixteen inches in diameter, which we tore into portions and used to scoop up our eggs. Later, we slept in our clothes on top of the mats. Once, in the night, I arose and went to the window. Shariff was climbing into his car. I watched him drive away and wondered why he had told us that the roads were too dangerous to navigate at night.

Leaving the next morning, we followed their directions and took the back road down the mountain in order to miss the police checkpoint. This took us through high mountain country where snow was still on the slopes, then down through the cedars of northern Lebanon, and back to the Mediterranean and Beirut. It was a beautiful day, but I was feeling edgy and tense and could only think of what lay ahead.

Dimitri must have been thinking the same thing. "I think we had better leave for London today, as soon as we get back into Beirut," he told me.

I looked down at my dusty white pants and sweaty blouse. My hair was dirty. I felt grimy all over—unclean. Suddenly the most important thing in my life was a bath.

"I can't go back to London looking like this. Let's spend the night and leave first thing in the morning."

He glanced quickly at me. "It doesn't matter what you look like. It's important to leave immediately. You know what I mean."

I knew exactly what he meant. But I was beginning to feel my skin crawl. I needed to wash, to clean myself up, to rinse the look of guilt away. Surely, I argued, we would have a far better chance in customs if we didn't look like this.

So we stayed the night. I bathed and rested and had my hair done. And in the morning I repacked my suitcase carefully and locked it. Dimitri left separately to go ahead of me to the airport, and I walked down the street to a little café to calm myself and collect my thoughts. No matter what, I couldn't let my nervousness show. When I went through customs, I had to make a good—an innocent—impression.

CHAPTER

7

"A good impression . . . an innocent impression." The words repeated themselves over and over in my mind.

I raised my head from the mat and rolled over on my side, leaning on one elbow and supporting my forehead with my hand. The room seemed to move—back and forth, back and forth—and little dots darted across my vision like black flies. My skin felt hot, and my throat was dry. I pulled myself to my knees, to my feet, then staggered and fell against the damp wall. I held myself there a few minutes and then tried to use my voice.

"Guard . . . guard. Please . . . somebody listen!" At last I heard footsteps. "Please," I begged, "I need to wash. I'm . . . I'm so sick." I couldn't say any more. The terrible vomiting had stopped, but I still suffered from diarrhea. I wanted so badly to be clean, to stand under running water, to rinse the filth of this place away.

When the guard finally came, he motioned for me to use the facilities in my cell.

"Oh, I can't. It's so dirty in here. Please take me some place where I can clean up."

He looked at me curiously, but he opened the door, took me to a restroom, and left me there with a sponge. The cool water and soap took away some of the filth, but not the ache that had been building up inside.

I splashed myself again and again with the cool water until it seemed that my mind was beginning to work again. "A good impression" . . . I had to make a good impression. I had to get hold of myself. I vaguely remembered someone telling me that the courts had closed early on Monday, before my case came up. But this was the next morning. Tuesday. I would probably appear before the magistrate today. I could not go back and lie down and close my eyes anymore. If I appeared in court looking like this, I wouldn't have a chance.

No matter how sick or scared I felt, I couldn't—wouldn't—let it show. I went back to my cell. I hadn't eaten for four days, and my arms trembled as I tried to brush my hair and put on a little makeup. I had to lean against the wall to steady myself.

When I looked up, I saw a Lebanese woman peering through the bars at me. She was rather short and stocky and wore thick glasses over eyes that blinked rapidly. She kept tugging at a white sailor cap that covered her reddish hair.

There was a large bag over her shoulder, and she carried a notebook.

She put her face closer to the bars. "Are you the American arrested Friday for smuggling hashish?"

"Yes."

"Do you have a lawyer yet?"

"No . . . no, I don't."

She nodded as if that was exactly what she had expected me to say. Then she fished in her purse, pulled out a card, and handed it in through the bars.

"My name is Mary Mathias. The American Embassy notified me that you were here. Sometimes I handle cases for them, and they thought I might be able to help you."

I read the card out loud. "Mary Mathias, Attorney-at-law."

She nodded again. "That's right, dear. And if you need a lawyer, I'll be glad to help. You'll be going upstairs pretty soon. But you don't have to say anything to the magistrate until you have a lawyer. They can't make you testify without one. Remember, I'm willing to help you if you want me."

She gave a quick little nod, turned, and disappeared down the corridor. I could hear her heels clicking on the stairs. I stood and looked at her card and wondered what to do. Dimitri had already said he was getting a lawyer. The kind who could get us out of here for sure. But what if something went wrong? I tucked Mary Mathias' card into a corner of my purse . . . just in case.

It wasn't long before I had another visitor. He

was an American, a kind-looking man, thin, with strong features. He came right up to the bars and called my name.

"Martha? Martha Sinclair?"

I went toward him. Only my mother called me by that name. He must have talked to her. A flood of relief washed through me. Marita had reached my mother. That meant that people at home were working to get me out of here.

"I'm Bob Paeth," he said. "I'm Crissy's brother."

Crissy Paeth was a friend back in San Francisco. I suddenly remembered that she had told me about a brother who taught at the American University in Beirut.

"Your mother called me last night and asked if I could help you. Are you all right? Is there anything you need?"

I couldn't seem to answer him. I leaned my head against the bars and tried to hold back the tears. He didn't touch me, but I felt comforted. A little of the tightness in my stomach eased.

He motioned toward a short, dark Lebanese who was standing behind him in the shadows. "This is the lawyer your mother told me to call," he explained. He didn't sound very enthusiastic.

The lawyer stepped forward where I could see him better. He wore a long black robe with a white pleated bib in front and held a black book in his hands. He reminded me of a character out of Dickens. He started talking at once, speaking rapidly in heavily accented English.

I tried hard to concentrate on what he was saying. He seemed to be explaining the whole Lebanese judicial system. "Your appearance today," he said, "is just a preliminary step. If the magistrate decides against you, then you will be held for trial."

For trial? What was this strange little man talking about? I held tightly to the bars, fighting a wave of dizziness and nausea. Everything seemed unreal—far away.

"And tell the truth," I heard him say. "That is the most important thing of all. Be honest with the magistrate. Tell him everything, just the way it happened."

I almost laughed. I could hardly remember what the truth was. My whole life had become a curious mixture of lies and truths.

I just couldn't imagine going before the magistrate and saying, "Yes, I'm guilty." That was the kind of truth that would get me in trouble. No, I was going to stick to the truth that Dimitri and I had devised together. "I'm innocent." That was what I was going to say. I'd said it so much already that I almost believed it.

A guard motioned for the men to move away. "It's time to go upstairs," he said. I heard the key turn in the lock, and the door swung open.

Dimitri and Alexandrou were waiting, still cuffed together, in the hallway. They were dirty and unshaven, their clothes rumpled, their hair hanging in limp, wet strands. I saw the look on Dr. Paeth's face and felt ashamed for Dimitri. "He isn't like this," I wanted to say. "Don't judge him by the way he looks now." But Alexandrou, I thought, looked just the way he really was.

We all went together up the stairs and into a hallway. A man from the embassy was waiting, and he came over to get my name. Mary Mathias was there, too. She reached out and took my hand, squeezing it tightly. "Remember, my dear, you don't have to say anything to the magistrate without an attorney."

A guard motioned impatiently for me to go with him into the magistrate's office, and Bob Paeth and the little Lebanese man in black were allowed to come with me.

The magistrate was sitting behind a large desk, waiting for us. When I approached him, he got an offended, almost disgusted look on his face, as if he were trying not to smell something bad. I looked around the room. I didn't smell anything. Suddenly, with a feeling of horror, I knew. The stench of B'abda was upon me. A simple sponge bath hadn't been enough to erase the filth of four days. I wanted to go away somewhere and hide in shame, but I had to stand there at attention instead—right in the middle of the room, where I could answer his questions.

"Tell us why you did this!" he ordered. "Why did you put hashish in your suitcase and try to take it out of the country?"

I hesitated, trying to decide what to say. If I didn't want to speak without a lawyer, which lawyer should I choose? The one Dimitri might pick for us? The dark little man who had come with Bob Paeth? The lady called Mary Mathias?

I knew that I didn't want to make Dimitri angry. But as far as I knew he didn't really have a lawyer for us yet. And I knew that I didn't trust the little man in the black robe. What about Mary Mathias? My head began ringing, and I felt faint. I couldn't think clearly. I needed time . . . more time.

"Miss Sinclair. Please answer the question."

My time had run out. I had to do something now. I remembered the words of Mary Mathias: "They can't make you testify without an attorney."

I spoke slowly, fumbling for each word. "This man . . . is not my attorney." I pointed to the little man in black.

Bob Paeth looked confused. "But Martha, this is the man your mother told me to call."

"Yes, I'm her attorney." The little man nodded vigorously.

The magistrate looked at me curiously. "Everyone says that this man is your attorney. What do you say?"

I shook my head. "He is not my attorney. I won't speak without my attorney."

The magistrate's voice was stern. "If you don't testify, Miss Sinclair, I will be forced to assign you to another day." He leaned forward. "You might have to wait for months. You don't want that to happen, do you?"

No, I didn't. But I didn't want this man to represent me, either. The more I saw of him, the less I liked him. And I didn't trust him at all.

"He's not my attorney," I insisted. "I haven't selected an attorney yet."

The magistrate shook his head. "Two days," he ordered. "Come back in two days with an attorney."

Dimitri and Alexandrou were called into his office separately. Then we all faced him together. The magistrate noted that the two men had told conflicting stories and that I would not testify at all. "Have you changed your mind?" he asked me.

I shook my head, and he dismissed us all with a wave of his hand. Bob Paeth left me as I walked back down the stone steps to the cells below. I tried to thank him, but I didn't know what to say. He had tried to help me, and I had refused. What did he think of me now? What did anybody think?

I sat on my mat and held my head. What was going to become of me? I could trust Bob Paeth. Somehow I felt sure of that. But would he ever bother with me again? I still had the card of Mary Mathias in my purse, but how could I call her when I was locked away in this cell?

I was still sitting there when a guard came and unlocked the door. "Get your things together," he told me. "You are leaving."

I quickly collected my clothes and stuffed them back into the sack outside. Then I put on my sun hat and sunglasses so that I felt camouflaged—safe from the stares of the people on the outside.

All the men who had been in the cell with Dimitri and Alexandrou were waiting in the hallway, standing in a line behind the guard. They were grizzly faced and dirty, and they smelled. Their chains rattled when they moved, filing slowly up the stairs. I followed behind, with another guard coming after me.

We went outside where a large truck was waiting. Four long wooden benches ran the length of the flatbed, and a green canvas canopy covered the top. The back was open, and the tailgate was about four feet from the ground. The guard motioned for the men to climb aboard and for me to follow them. No one offered to help me. I threw my sack into the back, and clambered clumsily aboard. A guard sat on either side of me.

I didn't know where we were going. It was just a bumpy road, down a hill. We passed houses on the side of the road, street vendors hawking fresh produce, and lots of people going about their daily living. It all seemed so normal. "Stop!" I wanted to scream. "Stop! Don't you see what's happening to me?"

Suddenly we were in Beirut, over the back roads, past the refugee camp. Finally we stopped, and I heard iron gates swing open. We drove through them, past a thick stone wall with an arched entrance. Inside was a courtyard and a huge, old stucco building with the plaster falling off. It had small, slit-type windows with bars—like a medieval fortress.

"Ramal!" I heard someone say. It was the men's prison. Everyone on the truck except me began climbing out. I watched Dimitri as he jumped off the back of the truck with the others.

He nodded as he passed me, his eyes going deep into mine. I raised my hand silently. Then he was gone.

I leaned out quickly to wave good-bye, but he never turned around. He followed the others, head down, shoulders stooped. I had never seen Dimitri look so beaten. My heart ached with pity . . . and with loneliness. They had taken Dimitri away, and I was afraid. Really afraid now.

The truck began to move, picked up speed, and was going faster now that it was lighter. We went down side roads that I had never seen before. The streets were crowded with people and vending carts. People hung from their windows and stood in the doorways. Their voices filled the air, rising and falling in an endless Arabic clatter.

We were heading for the Sanayeh district and the women's prison. The truck stopped in front of gates that opened onto an old yellow structure—a relic of a building, held over from colonial days. It was surrounded by walls and hemmed in by tall apartment buildings. I climbed down from the truck with a good deal of effort and was led through the gates and along a dirt path into a courtyard. There was a large green tree with some plants around it. I might have been entering the ruins of an old Spanish villa except for the guard who sat at a table in the corner.

He rose and led me up some stairs to double iron doors that were six feet tall, with open bars on top. He called out something in Arabic—

once, then again. Finally, there was an answer from the other side. Then I heard a key grate and turn in the lock. The door swung slowly open. The guards stepped back and motioned to me with their hands.

I walked slowly into the prison, alone.

CHAPTER

I was inside Sanayeh—the women's prison. I heard the door close behind me. There was nothing to do but step forward into the large, high-ceilinged room. It was a kind of foyer, with stark white walls, broken by windows with pointed Arabic arches.

I heard soft footsteps and saw a Bedouin woman approaching. She wore a scarf wrapped in a band around her head and a long, full robe that swished over the bare square bricks of the floor. She came directly to me, took my sack and purse, and began going through all my things. I felt violated, somehow, as I saw her hands reaching in and touching what was mine. She pulled each item out one at a time, looking it over carefully. Some things she put to one side, and others she returned, stuffing them back into the sack.

Every now and then she glanced up at me. Her

eyes were badly crossed, and a peculiar odor came from her clothes and skin. I thought she was indescribably repulsive.

When she was finished poking through my things, she led me around the corner into a dark hallway and began frisking my body. I held my breath, for I had put my watch and some money in my bra just before I got off the truck.

Her hands moved lightly, patting my clothes. Suddenly her fingers stopped. She reached inside my blouse, probed under my bra, and pulled out the money and then the watch.

We both stared at what she had found. She looked at me for a moment with her crossed eyes, then motioned for me to follow her into an office just off the corridor. A young Lebanese woman sat at a large desk leafing through some papers. She wore a white blouse with a blue skirt and tie and very large horn-rimmed glasses. Her fingernails were long and pointed and were lacquered bright red—almost the same color as the acne sores on her face.

She glanced at the watch and money that the Bedouin woman laid on her desk. "Why did you try to hide these things?" she asked.

Why? Why did she think? Because they were things I didn't want taken away. I needed my watch, didn't I? How else could I keep track of the time? And I had to have money. How was I going to live without it? I tried to explain—to tell her how I felt. But I only managed to say a few words before I started to cry. Deep sobs rose from within me—loud animallike cries that I couldn't seem to suppress. I pressed my palms tightly against my face, horrified by the sounds I was making.

A radio in the corner was blaring Arabic music, shrill repetitious sounds in a metallic, minor key. The music grated against my nerves as the strange dissonant syllables repeated themselves over and over, at first without meaning, then gradually seeming to become echoes of the harsh questions that were churning in my mind.

How was I going to survive in here? What were these people going to do to me?

The woman's voice rose, but it was not angry. "I will keep your money and put it into an account for you. You will be able to spend it on food and other things. Your valuables will be put into our safe." She motioned toward the large Bedouin woman and called her by name. "Rahaili has removed that which is forbidden from your sack. You may keep the rest." She pushed forward a paper and showed me where to sign. "I am Noha," she said. And she dismissed me with a twist of her head.

I followed Rahaili back into the foyer. My sack was over in the corner where she had put it after stuffing everything back inside. I was sure the contents were all in a mess, for I could see parts of clothing hanging over the edges. I picked it up in my arms and stood waiting to see what would happen next.

A dark-skinned girl was standing at the side of the room. She was quite pretty, with chestnut hair that hung long and straight over her shoulders. She wore a white Arabic robe and had long beads around her neck and sandals on her feet. She came toward me, smiling. "I am Lena. I will take you back to the foreigners' room."

I followed her through an iron door with heavy double screening—very strong, like a chain link fence—and then down a long hallway. We passed a heavy-set female guard who was sitting on a bench knitting. She didn't even raise her head.

On one side of the corridor was the outside wall with its few small, barred windows. On the other side were four doors with little metal peepholes that could only be opened or shut from the hallway side. But now the doors had been opened wide and swung back against the wall, so that I could look into the small, high-ceilinged rooms. They were dark and seemed very old. The plaster was peeling off in long, uneven strips.

Inside the rooms, a number of Arab women walked back and forth or squatted against the walls. Some were dressed Bedouin-style, and others were in rags. Their expressions were apathetic, their movements listless. Loudspeakers hung at intervals in the hallway, pouring out wailing Arabic music that mixed with the voices of the women in a strange, sad discord of sound.

The whole corridor smelled of the piles of garbage and uneaten food that littered the floor outside each room. Large, shiny cockroaches crawled over the debris and darted in and out of the cracks in the walls. The sight of them made me sick. How could I live in a place like this? I held my sack tightly, trying to stop the trembling in my arms. I couldn't go any farther. I just couldn't!

But I did. I found myself following Lena on to the end of the corridor, where it split like a *T*, going in two directions. We turned to the left and, a few seconds later, passed a large iron door that was open so that we could see out into a courtyard.

I paused and looked out at a great white wall that seemed to be about twelve feet high with barbed wire on top. Some of the prisoners were squatting against it, seeking the little shade that it provided against the hot afternoon sun. A few of them held nursing babies. Others stood in small restless groups or wandered aimlessly about. Some rested in the shade of a single large eucalyptus tree.

There were old women and young women out there, most of them in Bedouin dress, but a few with miniskirts and high-stacked shoes. All of them were talking loudly. A few children ran in and out among the women, shouting and playing and adding to the confusion of sounds. And always there was the music, blaring from the loudspeakers in a continuous noisy assault on my ears.

I didn't see any guards. They weren't necessary. Who was going to try to climb a twelve-foot wall with barbed wire on top? I felt a closed, tight feeling in my throat. For these women, there was no way out. And I was a prisoner, too. I was one of them.

Lena went to the end of the hall and stopped at the last door on the right. A pile of suitcases was stacked in the hallway next to a long green work table with a slanted desk top. Boxes of books were piled on the floor against the wall.

I looked in through the open doorway at the small, poorly lit room. It was overcrowded and smelled of mildew, bodies, and spoiling food. There was one window high on the wall. Half of it was open, for the glass on that side had long ago been broken. The other half contained glass, but it had been painted dark gray, so that no sunlight could pass through it. The dingy walls were a dull ocher color, partly covered with magazine cutouts like a half-finished collage. The floor had four mats side by side along one wall, and two more mats end to end along another. There was no place to walk except along a narrow strip between the mats to another door across the room.

Part of my view was broken by a long clothesline that was strung from the top bar of the only window and stretched across to the doorway. It sagged from the weight of the clothes piled on it, but they weren't wet. This was evidently some sort of open community closet. I saw a closed trunk in one corner that served as a table for baskets filled with fruit. A conglomeration of things hung from hooks placed haphazardly on the walls. A tilting wooden ledge held open jars of food and a number of cartons. I saw some peanut butter and cheese and coffee, and there were cups and dirty forks and knives. A large, three-inch cockroach moved quickly above the ledge, darted behind an open can of tuna fish, and disappeared.

I put my sack down and stood there nervously in the doorway while Lena introduced me to the girls who lived in the room.

There was Jenny who was from England and wore her fiery red hair frizzed out and down to her shoulders. She had on a long white Arabic robe with lots of beads and bangles around her neck and was busy doing yoga exercises.

Nicole was from Canada, a petite girl, except for her large breasts which seemed terribly out of proportion to the rest of her body. She wore a large *kefiya,* a Palestinian headgear made of black and white checkered material with deep fringe around the edges. She used this to wrap her entire body, sarong fashion, until it hung midcalf around her legs.

Over in a corner was a small, olive-complexioned girl who was Syrian, but came from France. Her name was Laila, and she spoke French and Arabic. I noticed that her hair was brown at the roots and blonde at the tips—some indication of how long she had been there.

Another girl came in through the door across the room. "That's the *loo,*" Lena told me. "You know, the bathroom. Aiya has been in there washing out clothes." Aiya gave me a little nod. She was from Russia—quite pale, with delicate features and short straight hair. She was wearing a tank top T-shirt and shorts and was very obviously pregnant. Lena told me that Aiya spoke Russian and German, but no English.

Verena was from Switzerland—a short, rounded type, quite pretty, with short brown hair. And Lena, who had introduced me, was from Denmark.

"That's it for room seven," Lena told me. "You can put your things here in front of the door. It's the only space we have left. It will have to be your spot until someone leaves."

I looked around at the faces that stared at me. There was no greeting, no welcome. Just mild curiosity, and then a casual indifference. Lena was the only one who showed any inclination to be friendly.

Their faces blurred, and I felt a buzzing in my head. Squatting quickly on the floor, I put my head between my knees. Everyone ignored me, and I stayed that way until my vision cleared and I felt as if I could stand up again. It was midafternoon, and I still hadn't eaten. I felt so sick—so tired. If only I could find a place where I could wash up—and then lie down.

"Is . . . is there somewhere I can go to clean myself up?" I asked.

Lena took me into the long narrow bathroom. On one wall was the shower, which splashed water onto the floor and into the plastic laundry baskets lining the wall, then drained down into the toilet, which was nothing but a basin sunk into the floor, with a water box above it on the wall and a chain to pull for flushing. On another wall there was a small sink, and at the end of the room was a big wooden cupboard full of plastic dishes and cockroaches. The women evidently toileted, showered, and washed their clothes and dishes all in the same room. A length of rope zigzagged from wall to wall for hanging wet towels and washrags.

The stench in the room was overpowering. I looked around to discover its source. In the corner by the shower were piles of dirty toilet paper and used sanitary napkins with black flies and large cockroaches crawling over them. When I thought of the open food on the shelf in the other room, I gagged and almost vomited.

I quickly turned on the cold water and let it run over my body, wishing that all the filth of this place could be washed down the drain with my own dirt.

A few moments later, Lena called to me from a tiny enclosed room on the other side of the bathroom. "Come on in here. We've got a surprise for you."

I didn't feel like any surprises. I only wanted to lie down and close my eyes and be left alone. But I was afraid I would offend them, so I walked to the door of the little room and looked in. All the girls were there, sitting in a circle on the floor.

"Welcome to the coffin," Lena greeted me. It *was* like a coffin—small and airless—but the other girls didn't seem to mind. Their eyes were all on Lena. She held up a small crocheted and beaded bag and waved it slowly in front of her as if she were displaying something precious. "Just look what I've got."

She opened the bag, and a now familiar smell drifted across the room. Lena took a pinch of hashish, placed it on a piece of paper, and rolled it into a cigarette. "Come on, sit down over there. You look as if you could use a smoke."

I didn't want to sit down. I wanted to get out of here right now. I was terrified of being caught with hashish again. But if I walked away, what would these women think of me? What would my life be like in here if I refused them?

"What about the guards?" I asked.

"What about them?" Lena taunted. "They never come in here to check us. Our room is too dirty. We get away with this every day. Smoking hash is our survival. It's the only way we can stand to be in this place."

They were all looking at me. I could see amusement on their faces. And something else. I was being tested. They had been watching me since I arrived. Watching and waiting. Now they were saying, "You're with us or against us. Take your choice now."

Oh, Dimitri. If you could see what's happening to me now!

I squatted down on the floor and held out my hand, taking the joint when it was offered. I tried not to inhale too deeply, remembering the effect hashish had had on me before. Then I passed it on and watched the others settle back, resting their heads against the wall. The small room was soon filled with smoke. A haze enveloped us. I seemed to be suspended in the fragrance. Where was I? I could barely remember. It didn't seem to matter anymore.

Suddenly I heard a loud buzzing noise and jerked my head around to see where it was coming from. No one else seemed to hear it. But it grew louder; it surrounded me, filled my mind, until there wasn't room for anything else but the terrible sound of it. It developed a rhythm—a beat—my head was pounding with pain.

"I've got to lie down." I looked slowly around the room. Whose voice was that? Had I spoken those words out loud? Cautiously I made my way toward the door, but it wouldn't seem to stop moving, fading in and out before me, bending and twisting in a grotesque dance.

What was wrong? What was happening to me? I had never felt like this before. "Sick . . . sick . . . I feel so sick. . . ." The voice was mine. I was talking to myself.

I reached the main room and took a pile of dirty, olive-colored blankets that no one seemed to be using. I dropped them on the floor and spread my red shirt over the top. I lay there with my eyes closed waiting for the buzzing to stop.

Once I heard someone moving near me and looked up to see Rahaili staring at me with her crossed eyes. She said something in Arabic that I couldn't understand. Then she was gone, and I heard the outer door slam. Someone kicked the latches into the floor, and there was the thud of a heavy padlock hitting the door.

We were locked in for the night.

CHAPTER

9

I moaned and closed my eyes tighter. Someone was shaking me, but I didn't want to wake up. My body ached from sleeping wedged up against the door, and my head still throbbed from the effects of the hashish I had smoked the night before.

The shaking persisted, and I was aware of the door jiggling against my back. Warily, I peered out through half-closed eyelids. The cross-eyed Bedouin, Rahaili, was trying to push her way into the room, and I was obviously in her way. I scrambled to my knees and shoved my bedding aside. I had slept in my clothes, and they were wringing wet. My skin was damp, too, covered with perspiration as if I had sweated out a fever. I got to my feet and stood there, feeling awkward and out of place. A young Arab girl who had been standing behind Rahaili handed me a big aluminum kettle full of steaming water.

They turned and left without a word, and I stood holding the hot kettle, wondering what I was supposed to do with it.

Everyone in the room was still sleeping, except Laila, who was sitting quietly on her mat, crocheting. She rose and pointed to a large thermos on the wooden ledge that held the open containers of food. Together we poured some of the hot water into it. Then she showed me how to wrap a towel around the kettle to keep the rest of the water warm.

There was a jar of instant coffee on the ledge. I looked at it and felt my stomach lurch. The thought of eating anything in this place repulsed me. But I had had no food for days, and I knew that I really didn't have any choice. Maybe if I made the coffee very weak I would be able to keep it down. I mixed a cup and sipped it slowly. My stomach cramped violently, and I had to rest between sips and wait for the pain to go away. Common sense told me that coffee wasn't going to be enough to live on. I needed something nourishing, and I needed it soon.

I inspected the food on the ledge to see what seemed to be the least contaminated, and chose a jar of peanut butter with the top still on it. Then I took a knife that didn't look as dirty as the others and spread a little on a cracker. As I reached for a peach, a long brown cockroach ran over the back of my hand and up my arm. I jumped back, brushing frantically at my skin, then saw another roach just like it on the peach I was holding. I stared in horror as the ledge began to move. It was crawling with the filthy bugs. They were down in the shadows behind the fruit and in the open cans of food.

Laila sat silently on her mat, still crocheting. But I noticed that she kept looking at me. Her eyes were curious—watchful. And it made me angry. I swore to myself that I wouldn't fall apart in front of her, and swallowed hard, trying not to gag. I could either eat or starve. So I bit into the peach and ate it slowly, determined to keep it down. It would only be for two days, I told myself. *Two days.* That's what the magistrate had said: "Come back in two days with your lawyer." I sat and sucked the peach and glanced furtively around the room at the sleeping bodies.

Suddenly, I noticed that the hand that held my coffee cup was red. So was my arm—and my shoulders. Bright red, like a terrible contagious rash that was slowly spreading over my body. What was happening to me? I touched my skin gingerly—I rubbed it hard. Then noticed the streaks that the peach juice had made down one arm—like sweaty water marks on dirty skin.

It was dye. Red dye!

I had perspired so profusely during the night that the color from my red shirt had rubbed off onto my skin. I began to laugh, and then to cry—silently, so that the tears ran down my cheeks and neck and made more streaks against the redness of my skin—but the girls in the room slept on.

Oh, I had to get out of here—out of Sanayeh!

This crowded room held no place for me. I didn't belong in a place like this. I didn't belong in prison!

I looked around the room at the sleeping bodies and at Laila, still sitting on her mat, watching me. And I remembered that when I had arrived the afternoon before, some of the girls had still been in their short nightgowns. They must have gone all day without getting dressed.

I wasn't going to be like them. I made a sudden, defiant decision. If I couldn't get out of Sanayeh, I could at least get out of this room for a while. I went into the bathroom and showered quickly, trying not to look at the piles of filth in the corner. Then I put on a blue wraparound skirt and a cool halter top. The skirt was long and fell to my ankles, covering my legs, and I was glad. It seemed, in some impossible way, to protect me from some of the filth of the prison.

I escaped to the slant-top desk in the hallway, borrowed some paper from another prisoner, and began writing letters home. Someone over there had to help me. Someone had to come and get me out!

I wrote for a long time, while the Arabic music wailed unceasingly from the loudspeakers in the hall, and the Arabic women walked aimlessly past me. Suddenly, I remembered the girl named Laurel who had spoken with me in the cell at B'abda. She had said I could ask for her when I came to the prison.

When two Arab girls appeared to collect the garbage, I began saying her name over and over.

"Laurel? Where is Laurel? Do you know Laurel?"

One of them pointed to the room next door and called her name loudly. "Laur-el . . . Laur-el. . . ." In less than a minute, she was standing in the doorway.

"Remember me?" I asked.

"Sure, I remember you. I thought you would be coming here."

"How did your trial go the other day?"

She shrugged. "Not too well, I guess. I'm afraid the judges didn't believe me." She walked over and sat down on the bench beside me. I thought she seemed more relaxed than she had been before—a little more willing to talk. She began tapping the table in a little rhythmic beat with a couple of chopsticks that she held between her fingers.

"I was picked up in customs carrying three kilos of pure heroin. They said it was the purest ever to enter Lebanon—worth more than a million dollars. The joke is, I didn't even know it was there. All the time I thought I was carrying secret documents for the Palestinians. But the judges just aren't buying that."

Laurel had come to Lebanon, she told me, as a representative of UNICEF to investigate conditions in the Palestinian refugee camps. She became a Palestinian supporter and agreed to carry important papers back to the States. She was given a locked suitcase and a round-trip ticket to New York, but she never even made it to the plane.

"Who's your attorney?" I asked.

"She's a woman—Mary Mathias."

"What do you think of her?"

"She's doing a good job for me. Right now, she's asking for a retrial. Oh, I know the girls in room seven don't like her—they think she's a little crazy or something. But she's the kind of person who really works hard for you if she thinks you're innocent."

I nodded, running that through my mind. I needed a lawyer, and I needed one in a hurry. If Dimitri didn't come up with someone soon, I was going to have to make my own arrangements.

Laurel seemed to sense my worry. "I can call her for you if you like."

Why not? If the other lawyer came through, I needn't worry. If not . . . Mary Mathias might be one answer.

We went together to Noha's office, and I listened while Laurel arranged to make the call. She spoke fluent Arabic, because she had been raised in the Middle East by missionary parents in Oman. I couldn't understand a word that she said, but I did notice that her Arabic sounded different from the rest. She spoke softly and sweetly, as if she loved the sound of the language. And I noticed Noha responding with a smile.

We went back to the bench in the hallway, but we didn't talk much more. Laurel seemed wrapped in her own thoughts.

At midmorning, big buckets of wheat boiled in olive oil were brought out of the kitchen into the main hall. The Arab women noisily lined up with their plastic bowls for the one meal of the day. The scene was like a prisoner-of-war camp, and the food smelled strange and unappetizing.

I looked at it once and told myself that I wasn't that hungry yet. Surely, for a day or two, I could find something on the ledge that wasn't full of roaches. Lena had told me to help myself to whatever I could find. There was always a supply of *lebana,* a kind of thick, soured milk, a little like yogurt. "And you can buy fruit and other food for yourself," she added, "as long as you have money in your account. Twice a week one of the Arab girls comes to take orders."

I nodded and thanked her, but I didn't think I would have to bother with ordering any food. I would only be staying here for a short time, and I could survive on light snacks for a little while. I wasn't planning on making this place a habit.

"Avuoka . . . avuoka." An Arab girl was standing by the table repeating the same words over and over and motioning at me with her hands. *"Avuoka!"*

I looked helplessly at Laurel. "What does she want?"

"You're supposed to go with her up front. Maybe someone has come to see you."

I nodded toward the girl. "I thought she was just another prisoner. Does she work here or something?"

"She's a trustee. Women like Rahaili, who are in for life sentences, are called trustees. They help the guards with their work, but they don't wear uniforms."

So, I thought, Rahaili, the cross-eyed Bedouin, was a prisoner just like me. I hadn't thought of her as a prisoner. There was something about her that defied this place—something free. For the first time since I'd come here, I felt a prick of curiosity about another person.

I followed the girl back down the main corridor, through the heavily screened door, and into a little room just off the main foyer. A young Arab sat on a bench, apparently waiting to see me. As soon as the trustee was gone, he handed me a note and waited for me to read it.

"This is my lawyer. I hope he will be yours, too. Love, Dimitri."

The Arab, who looked too young to be a lawyer, said that he was representing Ma'louf, Dimitri's attorney. "The minister is a busy man," he said. "I am going to do the footwork for him."

I suspected, from the inept way he questioned me, that he was only a law student or a clerk in Ma'louf's office. He didn't speak fluent English, and I spoke no French. It was a frustrating conversation. I tried to answer his questions. But all he would say in response to mine was that he would talk to the minister and see if Ma'louf could get us out. He would be back very soon, he said, but as I walked back down the corridor, I felt confused and discouraged.

When I turned the corner, I almost bumped into Rahaili, who was supervising the daily washing of the hall floors. I tried to brush quickly past her, but she reached out and put her arm on my shoulder, as if to comfort me. She spoke a few words in Arabic—soft words, not at all like the noises the other women made when they were talking together.

She looked almost attractive in a purple Arabic dress with gold needlework on the neck and hemline. Her hair was completely covered by a scarf that wrapped around her head and flowed down her back. She carried herself well, I thought, with her head held high. There was definitely something special about Rahaili. For a second, there was a spark of communication between us. Then she was busy again, supervising the girls who were covering the floors with water and grains of crude soap, then sweeping the brown suds down the hallway with straw brooms, working back and forth in a zigzag pattern. When they reached the door that opened into the courtyard, they swept the water down the steps and out into the dirt.

But the hall in front of room seven was not washed. They went right around it, leaving all the dirt and dust on the floor. Later, I asked Lena why. She shrugged and pointed to the piles of suitcases on the floor and the boxes of magazines and books pushed under the table.

"No one wants to bother to move those," she said. "And anyway, we don't worry about the dirt."

I worried about it. I hated it. But I didn't say anything, for they were the ones who were going to have to stay here and live with it.

I soon learned that the scrubbing process began every day at four o'clock in the afternoon, and lockup followed almost immediately afterward at four-thirty. It was still daylight outside, but the big wooden doors were pulled together. Heavy metal fasteners were banged into the doorframe with a distinct snapping sound. Then a bar was placed across the outside of the doors to secure the lock, and the huge metal padlock locked in place to hold the two sides of the door closed. The evening kettle of hot water was to be passed in through the tiny hatch in the door.

The hours between lockup and twilight moved slowly. After the sun finally set, the girls lit candles on low cardboard boxes next to their beds. That evening they were busy finishing their presents for Lily, a Lebanese woman in the room next door. Her birthday was the next day, and there was going to be some sort of party for her.

I watched Nicole thread tiny beads onto a necklace she was making. She specialized in really elaborate beadwork and had a cardboard tray with beads in little boxes. The girls called all handwork and any other work by its Arabic name *istagal,* which we pronounced "stiggle."

I watched her, fascinated, and listened to them talk. They seemed really excited about the party they were planning, and I wondered about the woman called Lily.

"Who is she?" I asked Lena.

"You'll meet her tomorrow, and then you'll see. She and Laurel are both coming over to stay all night."

Lily, she told me, was one of the few political prisoners in Sanayeh. She was a wealthy Lebanese who had negotiated a contract between the last administration and a missile company in France. When it was discovered that the missiles were faulty, no one in the new administration wanted to accuse an official of the former government. So Lily became the sacrificial goat. She had received a commission for her work, and it was promptly labeled a bribe.

"In Lebanon," Lena said, "it isn't illegal to take a bribe. But it is illegal to refuse to tell who gave it to you. If Lily would only talk, she would go free."

The commandant himself had brought Lily to the prison months ago. He had demanded that the old isolation room, *infarad*, be completely scrubbed out from top to bottom, even though it was very late at night when they arrived. And he stayed there with her to see that it was done correctly.

The conversation went on and on, then gradually grew softer and stopped. The candles went out, one by one, until at last there was only a little moonlight from the window high on the wall.

I lay on my mat and listened to the conversation until the voices were silent. Then I stared at the dark shadows on the ceiling and wondered if I would still be here tomorrow night to meet the woman, Lily. From the Arab rooms I could hear rhythmic clapping and singing and the sound of someone drumming on a plastic bucket. It was strange bedtime music, but I listened to it until I fell asleep.

CHAPTER

Thursday was visiting day. I could sense the excitement, even among the counterculture girls of room seven. Even though they claimed to care about nothing but their evening smoke, I noticed that they got up and got dressed and waited tensely to see if they would be called up front.

I felt excited, too, for I would be leaving. Perhaps today—tomorrow at the latest. I waited anxiously for the lawyer from Ma'louf's office to come and give me the news. Finally, about midmorning, I was called to the visitors' room.

It was the same place I had met with the young lawyer the day before, but since this was a regular visiting day, all the rules were being closely followed. Visitors came to the prison and stood in a line outside the door to the room. Any packages or gifts were given to a guard at the door, who passed them on to a trustee for inspection. Prisoners were called, a few at a time, and were allowed to come in and talk through a screened partition. The room often became crowded, and private conversations were next to impossible. Only an attorney or someone with a special pass could come through the screening.

I expected to see Dimitri's lawyer, and was surprised when I entered the room and saw Bob Paeth and a small, quiet woman with satiny blonde hair sitting on the green bench on the prisoners' side of the room. Noha was on duty, and she had evidently granted me a special favor by letting them through—perhaps because I was so new.

Bob introduced his wife, Jessie, who taught third grade at the American Community School. We talked a little about teaching and school experiences, and they offered to get me some things I would need in case I stayed a few more days. A T-shirt to absorb the perspiration at night, a small suitcase for packing, a clean blanket, and some toothpaste. But the conversation was strained and superficial. We were all thinking about the reason I was here—and we had different opinions about my release.

"I have to tell you, Marti," Bob said, "that your case doesn't look very good to me."

I shook my head. "I'm sure I'll get out," I insisted. "There were only four kilos in my suitcase. Most of the girls in my room were caught with fifty or sixty kilos of hashish. Besides, I didn't know it was there. I'm innocent. Dimitri will swear to that."

"But it was still in your suitcase, Marti," Jessie said. "And you were the one who was carrying it. In Lebanon, the amount doesn't matter. Only the deed."

I felt myself draw back from them. Did they believe me—or did they suspect the truth? They were so kind, and they were trying to help me, but I felt a vulnerability when I was with them. For some reason, Bob Paeth made it hard for me to lie.

But I had to lie, didn't I? How else was I going to get out of this mess?

I changed the subject and told them about the lawyer Dimitri had sent. "He seemed awfully young," I said. "I hope he knows what he's doing."

"What about that lady who was there at B'abda?" Bob asked. "I thought she said she handled cases for the American Embassy."

I nodded. "That's Mary Mathias. She gave me her card. One of the other girls called her for me. I thought it was a good idea—just in case."

Bob Paeth nodded. I wondered why it made me feel so happy just to have his approval. "If you want me to, I'll check with her for you." He looked at his wife, and they rose to go. When they said good-bye, I could feel their concern about what happened to me.

"Don't worry," I said confidently. "I'll be out of here in a few days."

Bob smiled kindly. "I hope you're right, Marti." But I knew they didn't believe it would happen.

That evening Lily and Laurel came to room

116

seven at lockup time. Lily was a thin, delicate-looking woman with graying hair. But that wasn't what made her different. She carried herself with a dignity and poise that could only come with breeding. Her speech and manners spelled wealth to the prisoners and guards. She commanded respect—and she got it.

She and Laurel seemed at ease together and were, I thought, much higher quality than the girls in room seven. How I wished I could be with them instead of here.

Lena was cooking a pot of wheat in olive oil. Laila and Jenny were preparing a fruit salad with *lebana* on the top. Someone had smuggled in a bottle of wine, which was definitely on the *memnua,* or forbidden list. And there was a store-bought birthday cake. Lily's birthday was to be a real celebration.

But now there were nine women in the twelve-by-fifteen-foot room. It was hot and crowded and noisy, and the floor was covered with wall-to-wall mats. I was uncomfortable and ill at ease, not knowing what to say or do. They all seemed to know each other so well, but I didn't really know anybody. I was among them—but not with them. It didn't matter anyway, I told myself. I would be getting out, and they would still be here.

I was sitting alone by the door, which was still the only place I had, when Lily approached me. "Let's go over in the corner where it's a little quieter," she said.

We took one of the mats with us and sat against the wall. They were sponge rubber, about two inches thick, and covered with rough gunnysacking. The heat was intense, and the mat made my legs itch. Lily took off her housecoat and wrapped a large towel over her bra and pants. I had to give her credit. She could dress like that and still manage to retain her dignity.

She had been in America several times, she told me. Her English was good, and I soon found myself talking to her easily, as if I'd known her for a long time. She listened with interest as I told her about my case. Her face was expressive, and I could tell that she was really absorbing what I said. Sometimes she interrupted to ask a question or clarify something she wasn't sure about.

"This really seems all wrong to me," I complained, "to be arrested and slapped in prison without bail."

She laughed. "This is not the British system," she told me. "The Lebanese operate under French law. You are guilty until proven innocent. It may seem strange to you, but that's the way it is."

No one had told me this before. All my protestations about being innocent hadn't meant a thing. I was automatically guilty. My heart skipped a beat. That meant I was going to have to prove I was innocent. But how? Would Dimitri's word be enough? More than ever I was beginning to see the need for a good lawyer.

I asked Lily if she had any advice. "Well," she said with a sigh, "one of the best ways to get out is to pay. Unfortunately, that isn't always possible. You're going to need a lawyer, Marti.

You're going to need a good one. But don't pay any lawyer ahead of time . . . even one you trust. Once they have your money, they won't do a thing for you unless you give them more . . . and more."

I leaned my head back against the wall and gave a little moan. "Oh, Lily, I'm so confused and lonely. You are the first person I've been able to talk to."

She was silent a moment. Then she reached out and patted me on the knee. "It's very crowded here in room seven," she said. "How would you like to move in with Laurel and me—for the few days you have left?"

I stared at her without speaking. Oh, the thought of getting out of this room—of being with someone who understood how I felt. I wanted to say, "Yes, yes. Oh, thank you, yes!" But what about Laurel? What would she have to say? I glanced over at her. She had headphones on and was listening to music while she wrote letters. Lily saw me and understood. "Don't worry," she said. "Laurel will think it is fine."

Late that night, I was awakened by the sound of screaming. High, shrill shrieks that split the hot air and sent the whole roomful of us scrambling to our feet. It was Lena, and she was white with fear.

"A rat!" she cried. "A big one, in the *loo.*" She wrapped both arms around herself and shuddered. "I went in there to go to the bathroom, and it came out and ran toward me." She shuddered again and added, "Where there's one rat, there's always more."

I wouldn't wait until tomorrow night, I decided. I would move into *infarad* first thing in the morning. There was no bathroom there, and we would have to use what the girls called "pee pots," and scrub them out each morning. But I didn't care. Anything was better than rats.

But when morning came, I didn't have a chance to think about moving. The young man from Ma'louf's office came early and called me to the visitors' room.

"Good news!" he told me. "It will be arranged for you to go free at the magistrate's level, and Mr. Strongilis will only get six months for smoking. This will cost you only one thousand Lebanese pounds."

One thousand pounds! Where was I going to get that kind of money? I knew Dimitri didn't have it. Maybe Leonidas. . . . But I felt myself shudder at the thought of him. He was one person I didn't want to get involved with ever again. I would have to ask my parents—and my friends. It would all take time.

The young man was pushing a paper at me. It looked like some sort of legal document. "Please sign," he said, and he tapped his pen on the dotted line.

I reached for it. "What is this?"

"Only a simple document. It is power of attorney paper. You must sign here." He tapped the page again. "It is necessary. Nothing can be done until you sign."

I hesitated. It was written in Arabic. How did I know what it said?

He grew insistent, almost indignant. "Mr.

Strongilis has already signed. You must sign, too, or I cannot help you." He folded his arms across his thin chest and waited.

I watched him for a moment. How did I know what Dimitri had really done? I hadn't trusted the lawyer in the long black robe at B'abda, and I didn't trust this impertinent little man, either. I put the paper on the table and pushed it away.

"I can't read Arabic," I told him. "I don't know what this says."

"It's all right," he insisted. "I will tell you. Now please sign your name."

He was pushing too hard. I shook my head and stood to go. His face flushed, and he reached for the paper and shook it at me. "This is a mistake," he warned me. "You are making a big mistake."

It was a relief to have him gone. I hoped that Dimitri wouldn't be angry. A few minutes later, I was called again. Bob Paeth was waiting in the visitors' room, and Mary Mathias was with him. "Nothing can be done until you choose an attorney," Bob told me, "and your mother has promised to wire Mary the money to represent you."

Mary held out a paper. It looked a lot like the one I had just refused to sign. "This is a power of attorney," she said. "I can do very little without it."

I hesitated. Everybody seemed to be pressuring me this morning. But I did need a lawyer, and Bob and my mother seemed to favor this one. My palms were wet and sticky when I finally picked up Mary's pen and signed my name.

"Good," she said. "Now I am going over to Ramal to see Dimitri Strongilis. I want to check out his story and verify what he is going to say."

Bob went with her. I thought, gratefully, that he was giving up a lot of his time for me. When they returned, it was just before lockup, and I could tell something was wrong.

"I don't know how you could stand to be around that Dimitri!" Mary was spitting out her words as if she could hardly bear to talk about him. "He's nothing better than an old shoe—and filthy besides." She climbed up on the guard's table and sat there with one foot on the chair in front of her and her hand against her knee. She looked directly at me as she spoke, and her voice was vehement.

"Let me tell you something, Marti. Your precious Dimitri didn't come back to the airport to help you at all. He saw what happened at customs, and he deserted you. He was picked up at Surete trying to get a new passport under another name so he could get out of the country."

I couldn't believe that! Dimitri would never desert me. Quick tears stung my eyes. I didn't want it to be true. Dimitri was the one person who really cared about me.

I looked toward Bob for support, but found none. "I'm afraid she's right, Marti. He is only interested in himself. Oh, yes, he agreed to stick with his story and say that you didn't know the hashish was there. But I heard him say, 'What does she want me to do—stay here and rot in prison?' Those don't sound to me like the words of a man in love."

"We won't speak anymore of Dimitri," Mary said with finality. "Your case is more important. Remember, you refused to speak last time you went before the magistrate, so we have to go back there again next week. That's the first step, and I need all the background information that you can give me."

Next week? I had been in Sanayeh since Tuesday afternoon. This was Friday, and I still wasn't out. "I thought he said two days," I said.

"He did. But that doesn't mean anything. You are scheduled for next week." She patted me on the arm. "Be patient, Marti. These things just take time."

I sat in the little room and tried to answer her questions. "How did you go to Yammoune? Why were you in Beirut? Describe the suitcase." On and on . . . with Mary always insisting, "I can't do my best, Marti, unless you tell me every bit of the truth. Now tell me once again!"

So I told her what truth I could and kept the rest to myself. When I went back to the room for lockup, I could think only about being here for another week. Seven days in this filthy place. Then I remembered. Tonight I was moving into *infarad*. I hurried, hoping it wasn't too late. Rahaili was ready to lock the doors, but I had time to snatch my few belongings and take them to the room next door.

Lily had the only elevated bed in the prison, except for the guards. Her own mattress from home was supported by three wooden benches. A white wicker table stood at one side, and a long shelf hung on the wall above the bed. The

123

room seemed neat and clean, and clothes hung from hooks on the wall rather than from a clothesline. In the far left corner, I saw a tape recorder and boxes of tapes and books.

I put my things in the far right-hand corner, and Laurel and I arranged our mats against the outside wall so that a good amount of open space was left to walk around in. Even though the window in this room had no glass, and a fine, brown dust was blowing in, I felt cleaner than in the other room. There was a peaceful feeling here in *infarad* that was hard to describe. I thought I might be able to survive the long week ahead if I could just stay here in this room with Lily and Laurel.

CHAPTER

11

For the next several days, Mary worked with me almost constantly, asking questions, taking notes, planning exactly what I should say. She met with Dimitri's lawyer so the two of us would have our stories straight, and she went to see Alexandrou's lawyer, too, to find out how he would be pleading.

She was working hard, and I was grateful. "I know you are innocent," she would tell me again and again. "You don't belong in this terrible place. I know you have told me the truth, Marti. I believe in you, and I will do everything in my power to get you out of here."

But I wasn't innocent, and I hadn't told her the truth. Yet I needed all the help I could get, and I didn't want my lawyer to turn against me, I rationalized. Anyway, it was better for Mary to think I was innocent. She was happier that way.

The first week of July, Dimitri, Alexandrou,

and I went back to B'abda and appeared before the same magistrate we had seen just after our arrest. Bob Paeth was there with Mary, and so was the man from Ma'louf's office, representing Dimitri. Alexandrou had his attorney from the Greek Embassy. We were, I thought, quite an international group. And I was excited, because I was sure I would be going home after this was over.

My timing was still right. I had told my board at The Bridge that I was going to be gone for six weeks, and I still had until the second week of July. There was no reason why I wouldn't be released in time if we worked really hard to get this thing cleared up. I would fly to London, then directly home, and I would wait there for Dimitri to get his freedom. I was ready—anxious—for the hearing to begin. I even imagined how I would tell my story to my friends at home. It would sound like a real international escapade.

But when they brought Dimitri in, I shuddered and stifled a sob. His hair had been cut off close to his scalp, and he wore a wrinkled shirt and the same dirty, sweaty pin-striped suit that he had been arrested in. He looked . . . like a criminal.

"Oh, Dimitri . . ." I whispered, still loving him.

I saw the look of disgust on Mary's face. She was too hard on him, I thought. Look how he had suffered! I longed to touch him—to feel his hand on mine. But there was no way I could go to him. We could only look at each other across the room.

It was time for the hearing to begin. The magistrate sat behind his big desk and asked questions while we stood at attention before him. Every word counted that day. If we slipped up— if our stories conflicted in any way—if the magistrate wasn't completely satisfied—then we would be charged with smuggling hashish and would have to wait for a court trial.

He spoke to each of us in turn, mostly asking questions that we had heard before. Dimitri was still claiming that he and Alexandrou had bought the hashish for personal use—for smoking. Alexandrou shook his head vehemently. "I know nothing about any of this," he insisted.

The magistrate looked at Dimitri. "Four kilos," he said. "That's two apiece. Quite a lot of hashish for personal use."

Dimitri nodded. "Yes, it is. But we didn't intend to make another trip. We wanted a good supply."

"Then why does your friend here deny being involved? One of you has to be lying." He looked at the two men for a long minute, then turned to me.

"Miss Sinclair, I would like to clear up a few details that seem a little confusing."

I nodded, feeling confident. Mary had tutored me well, and I was ready for his questions.

"You say that you went into the mountains to Yammoune on an overnight sightseeing trip. Is that correct?"

"Yes, sir."

"And no one stopped you? You saw no police or anyone else who tried to keep you from driving up to the village?"

"No, no one." I wondered what he was getting at.

He was looking at me intently. "That seems very strange, Miss Sinclair. Do you realize that I myself cannot go to Yammoune? The roads are so heavily guarded that no one can get up there . . . unless, of course, they know how to make illegal arrangements. Is that what you did, Miss Sinclair? Did the three of you make illegal arrangements so you could drive through to Yammoune?"

"No! Of course not."

"Then why do you suppose they let you through?"

I didn't have any answer. I had told him the truth. We had driven straight to Yammoune that day without any problems. And now I was wondering how we had done it, if it was as difficult as the magistrate said. Dimitri hadn't told me anything about special arrangements. Perhaps he had made them without my knowledge. Surely the magistrate could see that this only added more weight to my plea of innocence.

He consulted some papers on his desk, shifting through them as if he were looking for some note he had made earlier. "Ah, yes. . . ." He read for a moment, then looked up at me again. His eyes were dark and piercing, and I felt as if he could look right through me and pick out all the little indecisions and lies in my mind. I was going to have to be firm—really firm—when I answered him next.

"Now, Miss Sinclair, did your fiancé leave your room that night in Yammoune?"

The question was a surprise. But I was determined to answer it quickly, not to show any hesitation. Without thinking, I blurted out the truth.

"No. No, he didn't."

"Then how did the hashish get into your suitcase?" There was a little smile on his face. He looked almost amused. "Miss Sinclair, you have testified that your suitcase was left in the car all night, and your fiancé has admitted that he was the only one who had an extra set of keys. How do you suppose he managed to open the suitcase and put the hashish in it if he was in the room with you all the time?"

"I . . . I don't know." My voice broke, and I paused to regain control. What had I done? Of course Dimitri had to have left me sometime in the night! Otherwise, how could I be innocent? I should have said "yes" or "I don't know because I was sleeping." I said it now.

"Maybe . . . maybe he left me when I was asleep. That must be what happened."

"That's exactly what happened!"

It was Dimitri's voice, strong and loud. He sounded like himself for the first time since that awful day at the airport. "I waited until she was sleeping, and then I went out to the car. I've already told you she didn't know anything about it. Alexandrou and I put the hashish in her suitcase while she was still asleep."

I looked at him gratefully. But the magistrate was tapping his pencil on the table impatiently and looking through his papers once more. I wondered if Dimitri had managed to convince him.

I was glad when it was all over and Mary came up to reassure me. "Don't worry, Marti," she said. "Everything is going to be all right." But when I glanced at Bob Paeth and saw the worry in his eyes, I wasn't so sure.

It took seven more days for the magistrate's report to be completed. Seven whole days of waiting in Sanayeh. Would I be going home in seven days? I was sure of it during my waking hours when I talked to Lily and Laurel and listened to their encouragement. It was the only believable thing that could happen.

But at night, when I lay on the floor on my mat, I lived again that day in the magistrate's office, listened to my own stammered answers, and watched the expression on the magistrate's swarthy face. Then I grew frightened, for it seemed to me that he must know the truth.

When his report was finally delivered, it was even worse than I had expected. The magistrate had not only seen through my lies, but he had imagined that there was much more to the story.

Because all our stories conflicted—because Alexandrou and I constantly denied knowing anything about the hashish—and because Dimitri had obviously changed his story to protect me—the magistrate assumed that we were part of a much larger operation, a smuggling ring headed by Leonidas. He called it a "Greek Connection." A warrant was issued for the arrest of Leonidas, and our file was sent to the prosecutor.

"What does it mean?" I asked Mary. "What's going to happen to me now?" It was the middle of July. I should be packing. It was time to be getting ready to go home.

"Just a little delay," she assured me. "We will appeal to the Chambers of Accusation. They can overrule the magistrate's report."

Or they could agree with it, I thought. Then I really would have to stand trial. I didn't want to think about that. It had a terrible sound. For I knew that two things were undeniably against me: the hashish had been in my suitcase, and Dimitri had originally said that I knew it was there.

The appeal was made, and the wait began. Dimitri fired his lawyer and hired a new one, a lean, hungry-looking Arab who immediately came to see me with a note from Dimitri.

Though I had just received a letter from Mary urging me to forget him, I opened his note eagerly, anxious to see his handwriting—to read his words of love.

"My sweet love Marti . . ." he began.

Tears came to my eyes. The others were being far too hard on him, I thought. They didn't know him as I did.

"He wants to hear from you," the attorney said. He pushed a piece of paper toward me. "He is a very sad man." Then he told me that Dimitri was almost out of money and had not been able to contact his father and brother for more. "You can help him, yes? You can pay some of his bills?"

I hardly had enough money for my own expenses. How could I pay Dimitri's bills, too? But I remembered how he had stood up and defended me in front of the magistrate, and how he looked as though he had suffered more than I. And I remembered our days—and nights—of loving.

"Yes . . . I will help him," I replied, and I scribbled a short note saying that I would try to help him with some of his legal expenses. Then I signed my name.

The attorney smiled and pocketed the note. "You have filed today with Chambers of Accusation?" he asked pleasantly. "Today is last day."

Mary was taking care of everything for me. She must have filed. But she hadn't said anything about it. What if she had forgotten? The distress must have shown on my face.

The attorney pointed to himself and grinned happily. "I do it for you. I represent you and Mr. Strongilis together."

"No . . . no, I have my own lawyer. I'm sure that she has already filed."

But had she? How could I be sure? I left the visitors' room and ran to the office. The guard on duty was *Sit* Marie, who spoke no English. Using sign language, I motioned for her to call the number on Mary's card. She finally understood and dialed the telephone. There was no answer.

I was close to panic. Everything would be lost

if Mary had forgotten to do this one thing. I would have to stay here longer—maybe even weeks—waiting for a court trial. Bob could help. But I would have to find someone who could talk to him in English, because I wasn't allowed to speak on the phone.

I ran through the prison halls, searching for a guard who could help me. Finally I saw an Arab priest visiting the women in room six. He spoke a little English and was able to say enough on the phone so that I was sure that Bob understood. I relaxed. Everything would be all right now. Bob would know how to get ahold of Mary.

But the next morning they both came to see me, and they didn't look happy. Mary sat in her usual place on the table with one foot on a chair and began talking the minute I entered the visitors' room. "First of all," she said, "I am a little disappointed, Marti, that you felt you couldn't trust me completely. I told you I would file, and I did. I do not forget details like that. But that is not the reason I am here."

Her voice rose, and there was tightly suppressed anger in her tone. "I am here to tell you that you must choose between yourself and Dimitri. Right now, before it is too late!"

I stared at her blankly. What could have happened? The look in her eyes made me tremble. "I . . . I don't understand."

Mary lowered her voice. "Do you know about yesterday?" I shook my head. The only thing that had happened yesterday was the visit from Dimitri's lawyer.

"That pig! That new lawyer of Dimitri's. He

called me last night. He had a note that was signed by you. I saw it myself. Marti, I can hardly believe you would write such a thing, saying that you are willing to pay Dimitri's expenses *if* he continues to swear that you are innocent. He threatened to show it to the judges. Do you realize what that would mean? You will be ruined, Marti. Ruined!" She threw up her arms in disgust and kicked the chair in front of her so that it fell over and hit the floor with a crash.

"But I didn't . . . I really didn't write that! I just told him I would try to help Dimitri with expenses, because the lawyer told me he was having such a hard time getting money. I didn't see what else I could do. But I didn't ask him to do anything in return. You've got to believe me. I didn't!"

I looked to Bob for reassurance, but his usually tanned face was white and drawn.

"Bob had to give me one hundred pounds to pay the lawyer off!" Mary snapped. "He had to participate in bribery because of your indiscretion."

"Oh, Bob." I didn't know what to say. The expression on his face showed me how much this had hurt him. I felt terrible.

Bob and Jessie had both come faithfully to see me, bringing supplies, even making homemade bread. If they suspected I was guilty, I didn't know it, because they still kept coming, so often that the Arabic guards decided they must be my uncle and aunt. No friends, the guards said, would do so much. The bread, which Bob made himself, became known as "uncle's bread," and soon even the other prisoners began calling him "Marti's uncle."

How could I tell him how I felt now—how much I appreciated his friendship and how I hadn't done this on purpose? "Bob," I said, "I'm so sorry. You know I wouldn't hurt you or Jessie. Please, you have to believe me—you and Mary both. The note I wrote to Dimitri must have been altered. The lawyer changed it to suit his own purposes."

He nodded. "I believe you, Marti. I know you had good intentions, but. . . ."

"But good intentions are not enough!" Mary interrupted, still angry with me. "You must never talk to anyone else about your case," she insisted. "No more letters to Dimitri or meetings with his attorney. Promise me."

I promised. But it seemed to me that Dimitri and I were being forced further and further apart by events, by the people around us, by things we couldn't control.

The next day, Dimitri's attorney came to see me again. I appealed to Lily. "I promised not to talk to him. What shall I do?"

"I'll come with you," she offered. "I can tell him in Arabic that you won't talk to him. I will make sure that he understands."

He understood, and he was livid. "I tell this to Dimitri!" he shouted. "He know you not love him!"

A letter from Dimitri came quickly. An angry letter, saying that Mary was trying to force us apart, claiming that I didn't act as if I cared about him any longer. I put it aside and tried not to think about it. Just a little longer, I kept thinking. The report would come back from the Chambers of Accusation. The magistrate's decision would be overturned, and I would be free. Then I could visit Dimitri, and we would straighten everything out.

July 26 arrived, and the report came. But the judges who heard our appeal didn't overturn anything. They rubber-stamped the magistrate's report, and sent our case directly to the prosecuting attorney for trial. We were, in their opinion, guilty without a doubt.

Along with the report was a new statement from Dimitri's lawyer. Dimitri no longer supported my innocence, he said. He had changed his story and now claimed that I knew about the hashish and had agreed to carry it. Now there was little doubt in anyone's mind that I had been involved.

I was stunned by the report, but devastated by Dimitri's actions. Why had he done this to me? What had he hoped to gain? They had tricked him, I told myself. They had told him lies about me, and he had believed them. If only I could have talked to him. If only . . . if only. . . .

"Never mind," Mary kept telling me. "You will go free. It is just a matter of time, Marti. The court trial will come, and you will be released."

But the trial would not come soon, for the courts closed in August for summer vacation and remained closed throughout September, the annual month of fasting called *Ramadan*—the hot month. The court schedule for October was already filled with the cases of those who had been arrested in April and May. The earliest trial date we could possibly have was November 2.

"But this is still July," I wailed. "That means I will have to spend three more months in this horrible place!"

Mary patted me on the arm. "It cannot be helped," she said. "We are all doing our best for you. It is just a matter of time, Marti. Just a matter of time."

CHAPTER

12

I spent the next days thinking about what Mary had said. "A matter of time, Marti. Just a matter of time." Three months until the court trial, then what? More time?

I could go free or—I had to face it—I might stay in prison. The sentence would be three years if I were found guilty, with a possible amnesty after eighteen months.

Eighteen months in this place! I shuddered at the thought. Even if I could stay in *infarad* with Lily and Laurel, I couldn't imagine eighteen months of it. Eighteen months of living with filth and vile language and . . . and prison people!

But there was something that bothered me even more. I would come out of here with a record, and it would follow me for the rest of my life. How would I find another job in the States? Americans were not as tolerant of drug records as Europeans were. And what about my family—my friends? Who would ever want to marry me? What would I tell my children? Even if I were finally pardoned, people would always wonder. They would always see me as an ex-criminal. I would forever be on the fringe . . . never quite respectable.

I didn't feel good about myself—or about Dimitri. I didn't feel good about anything. But there were some things I had to do.

I wrote to my board of directors and suggested that they look for another administrator. I notified my parents of the delay and gave them the date of the court trial. I arranged for character references to be sent to Mary from agencies that were familiar with my work. And then, because I felt so lonely, I wrote letter after letter to friends at home, begging them to write back to me. I was so afraid that I would be forgotten. That I finally would go home, and people would say, "Marti? Marti who?"

My twenty-seventh birthday came and went, and there was a card from my mother that read: "A birthday is your own personal new year—your private mark in time between the past and future." I held it and cried, for I knew I was making no mark in time. I was simply marking time, day by day, and there seemed to be no past or future for me at all.

Sometimes I would take a pencil and some paper and try to draw, sketching my corner of the room, or the courtyard. Occasionally, I would try to capture an Arabic face that interested me. But most of the time it was idle doodling, without much point or purpose.

Then one day the shout went up—"Esther's here! Esther's back from vacation!" All the foreigners rushed up to the visitors' room and crowded around an American woman in a loose-fitting trench coat. Her hair was silver, and she wore glasses. But what I noticed most was the gentleness about her, the tender expression on her face. Everybody seemed to be trying to hand her something at once, but she didn't seem a bit ruffled and spoke to each of the girls by name.

I turned to Laurel. "Who is she? What's everybody so excited about?"

"She's Esther Horner. Her husband, Norman, teaches at the Baptist Theological Seminary in Beirut," Laurel explained. "He's doing research on the Orthodox Christian Church in the Middle East, and Esther has taken on the foreign girls here in Sanayeh as her special responsibility. She comes to see us on visiting days. She's our contact with the outside." She gave me a quick look. "Esther is all right."

I watched the woman distribute letters and packages from home that had been mailed to her house so the girls would be sure to get them. There were also Arabic sweets, small gifts from herself, books to be shared, and special purchases they had asked her to make.

One of the girls told me Esther would mail our letters for us, so I ran back and got some I had written. Then I just stood there watching and holding my letters and not knowing quite what to do until Laurel noticed me and said, "This is Marti."

Esther pushed up her glasses and smiled. "Hi, Marti." Only two words, but I felt warmed and comforted. There was no disapproval in her voice—no censure—not even curiosity. Her face seemed open and friendly, and I felt as if I could relax and be myself.

She gave me her address and said that I was welcome to use it for mail. Then she offered to contact my family if I ever needed something special. I gave her the letters, and then someone else claimed her away from me.

I soon learned that there was no way for everyone to talk to Esther privately in the short time she was allowed to visit, so the girls wrote letters, telling her of their concerns and problems and including lists of whatever they needed. She would answer each one personally, answering questions or giving advice.

Every time a girl had a birthday, Esther brought a three-layered cake—lemon, chocolate, angel food—always different. And she cooked sausage and ham and liver and brought it for no special reason, except that she thought we would enjoy it. She kept Nicole supplied with beads for her projects and was always looking out for creative things to keep us busy. Occasionally she was allowed to come back to our rooms where she could spend a little more time with us. I began to look forward to her visits.

I began to try to establish some sort of daily routine for myself. In the mornings, Lily and I did yoga together, our eyes shut, our hands uplifted in the lotus position, relaxing, and escaping briefly before we began another long day.

Laurel spent her mornings in room six with Alia, a friend of Rehaili's. She often visited with the Arab women and even with the *ra'eb,* an army sergeant who directed the prison.

On visiting days—Thursdays and Saturdays—Laurel and Lily were called forward many times to the visitors' room. But I was seldom called now, for the Paeths were on vacation, back home in the States, and my only contact with the outside world was an occasional visit from Tom Griffith, a friend of theirs, and a counselor at the American High School in Beirut.

So I appointed myself commissary for the food that Lily and Laurel received almost daily from their visitors, taking the bags from the trustees, removing what we needed, and distributing the rest as Lily and Laurel wished.

Food became my major preoccupation from the moment in the morning when Rahaili cried out, *"Shay, kahwa, zabali!"* ("Tea, coffee, garbage!") All the foreigners were allowed to use the prison kitchen to prepare their own meals, since we were not used to the Arabic foods. And if you were like Lily and Laurel whose friends kept them pretty well supplied, or if you could afford to order food from the outside, you didn't have to eat the prison food at all.

I hated the thought of eating the nasty-looking wheat cereal and thin soup that was served once a day to the Arab women who couldn't afford any better. I worried and fretted constantly, counting fruits and vegetables and eagerly commandeering the bags that came from visitors. What if we should run out of shopping money?

What if the food stopped coming in?

Lily offered to teach me to cook Lebanese dishes, so every afternoon I followed her into the kitchen to prepare our evening meal—usually a large *tabbula*—a salad of parsley, wheat, and tomatoes mixed with olive oil and lemon juice.

Only after dinner was served on the plastic cloth that we spread out on the floor, and the conversation and soft candlelight blurred the prison walls around us—only then did I feel that I had made it safely through another day.

One day I happened to pick up a poetry book that had been donated to the prison by some missionaries. It was written in English, and when I began to scan it, I saw a quote from the Bible:

> *Put away anxious thoughts about food and drink to keep you alive, and clothes to cover your body. Surely life is more than food, the body more than clothes. . . . No, do not ask anxiously, "What are we to eat? What are we to drink? What shall we wear?" . . . because your heavenly Father knows that you need them all. . . . So do not be anxious about tomorrow; tomorrow will look after itself. Each day has troubles enough of its own* (Matthew 6:25-34, NEB).

I copied it down and taped it above my bed. The words tantalized me, like a mirror held close to my innermost mind. It described the way I felt—full of anxious thoughts about physical things, full of worry about what tomorrow might bring.

I read the words again and again, hoping they would soothe me and take my tensions away. I tried to remember how it had been when I was a child and all those worries had been taken care of for me—the contentment I had felt when I had lived at home and our family had been a happy one. I tried to recapture it all, to find the peace I needed.

But I couldn't. If God knew what I needed, so did I. I needed to get out of here. If he was going to take care of me, when was he going to begin?

I continued to fuss about the food and began compulsively working off some of my nervousness by cleaning and organizing.

I cleared out the boxes and suitcases under the table outside our room so that the corridor could be scrubbed completely. On Sundays Laurel and I took everything out of *infarad* and washed the floor, cleaning the entire room. Then I organized and reorganized all my belongings in the corner by my mat, putting them first one way, and then another.

"Stiggle," the others called it. It was what Marti did all day long—work, work, work!

The only time I relaxed was during the noon hours when I lay on a blanket in the courtyard and sunbathed with the girls from room seven. The hot Beirut sun warmed my body and eased my muscles. I could close my eyes and pretend that I was on the beach at home, and, for a few hours, the prison seemed bearable.

But at night, when the door closed tightly and

we were locked in, I lay on my mat and began to imagine that there wasn't enough air to breathe in the little room. The heat was like a heavy weight pressing on my body. The tears would come, rolling down my cheeks, mixing with the sweat on my skin.

Why? Why did this have to happen to me? How could God have let it happen? I remembered something Jim had asked me long ago: "Well, if you believe in God, what can he do?" I hadn't been able to tell him then, and I sure didn't know the answer now. I was only certain of one thing. God was silent in Sanayeh.

August passed, and September came. *Ramadan* was here, and the Arab women chattered about it in the halls, planning the festive meals they could indulge in after the sun went down each day.

Suddenly, Lily was released. She was going to have to pay an exorbitant fine in monthly installments, but she would be free. I was happy for her, but fearful for myself, for this meant change. Would more prisoners be moved into *infarad*, or would I be sent back to room seven with the other foreigners? Whatever happened, it would not be the same. The peace of *infarad* would be ending, and it was two whole months before my trial.

CHAPTER

13

September began as a quiet month. The Paeths had returned and were visiting me regularly once again. Mary came too, bringing Arabic sweets and encouragement. "You'll be acquitted, Marti, darling. You'll see," she told me.

Letters arrived from home, and I wrote an equal number back, waiting anxiously for them to be answered. So far, Laurel and I had been allowed to stay in *infarad,* and we counted our blessings, even when two prostitutes came to share the room with us for a few nights.

Laurel had started a research project which she worked on daily—a kind of sociological study of prison life. She was interviewing, taking notes, and even going about measuring floors and walls in preparation for a scale diagram of Sanayeh. In the evenings we would talk about what she had learned that day. Because Laurel spoke Arabic, she was able to pick up all the undercurrents in the life of the prison—the conflicts, the hopes, and the deceits. "There isn't anything about this place that we don't know," I told her.

I did the cooking, as Lily had taught me, and Laurel did the washing up. "Do you mind, Marti?" she asked. "Maybe we should trade off."

I shook my head. It was an arrangement that pleased me. Even though cooking was more work, it kept me busy—gave me something constructive to do besides washing the floor and rearranging the mats and boxes.

I grew to enjoy the quiet moments in the morning, before the prison hubbub began. That was when I would squeeze a lemon into a cup of hot water and sip it slowly, waiting for the sun to warm the cold walls.

In the mornings, Laurel went to visit Alia, her special Arab friend, who lived in the same cell with Rahaili. Sometimes I went with her to drink Arabic coffee and eat a little bit of Arabic breakfast: bread that was spread with *zapher* and olive oil, scrambled eggs with sugar, black olives, green tomatoes, and occasionally a sweet dip of sesame seed paste and molasses, called *tahina*.

To fill my time, I began offering to cut hair for the other prisoners, and before long they came to me, foreigner and Arab alike, whenever they needed a trim.

One night, after Lily had left us, Laurel and I were both invited to room six to enjoy a *Ramadan* feast and spend the night with Alia and Rahaili. As soon as the sun had set, a red plastic tablecloth was spread out in the middle of the floor and dishes of Lebanese food were put out for everyone to share.

I was familiar with most of the foods after working with Lily in the kitchen. Still, I was amazed at the variety of the meal: *kafta*—cakes of ground lamb and wheat filled with sour cream; *lubya*—green beans boiled in olive oil and tomato juice with onions; the usual *tabbula* (salad); *hommos*—garbanzo beans pureed with lemon juice, garlic, *tanney* sauce, and olive oil; and soft round pieces of Arabic bread. For dessert, there was *baklava*, a pastry filled with nuts and honey, followed by cups of rich, dark Arabic coffee.

I couldn't understand most of the conversation, for my Arabic was limited to such easy phrases as *kayfa halik?* (how are you?), *n'am* (yes), and *la* (no). When any of the women spoke to me, Laurel translated what was said.

I watched Rahaili as she and Su'ad, the head kitchen girl, organized the cleanup. Rahaili supervised the prison in general, and Alia helped her by attending to the chores Rahaili didn't have time for—things like mending and cooking. Both Rahaili and Alia had been falsely accused of murdering their husbands. They were convicted and sentenced to long terms in Sanayeh and had been able to survive for seven long years, mainly, I thought, because of their concern for each other.

That night the mats were squeezed together so that fourteen of us could sleep together in the small room. No one played music or talked aloud, as they did in room seven for most of the night. It was still, quiet, and peaceful. I lay on the mat looking out at the sky through the barred window, and eventually went to sleep. It seemed, after all, that life in Sanayeh might be bearable.

But a cockroach woke me early the next morning by walking across my leg. It was still dark in the room, and the other women were all asleep. I reached for my shoe and killed it without waking them. It was a big roach, dark and juicy. I looked at it in the moonlight and shuddered, and I felt glad that it was dead.

The peacefulness of the room seemed broken, even though no one made a sound. A few minutes later, the early morning silence of the rest of the prison was shattered by the ominous call that echoed down the halls.

"Maa' fi my! Maa' fi my!" ("There is no water! There is no water!")

We had to stand in line to carry it in pails back to the rooms for washing, bathing, and flushing. It dribbled slowly out of the faucets, while the women pushed and pulled and fought for their places in the line.

"What will we do if we run out?" I whispered to Laurel. I kept remembering the roach I had killed that morning and how it had felt crawling on my leg. If we didn't have water for scrubbing and cleaning, the roaches would have a heyday. I looked frantically for an extra pail to fill.

That was the day that my face began to break out. "Look at me!" I wailed to Laurel. "I look so ugly!" She couldn't argue with that. My skin was

149

red and scabby and covered with patches of pimples. I stared at myself in one of the little hand mirrors that we were forbidden to have, but kept anyway. For the first time, I was glad that it wasn't time yet for my court trial. I didn't want to be seen in public looking like this.

Slowly, the quiet routine that Laurel and I had enjoyed began to erupt into chaos, both inside the room and out. The peace of *infarad* was ending, just as I had feared.

Early in October, Suzanne arrived. She was an American who had been in Sanayeh one night in August, then was taken to the prison hospital with typhoid. She was terribly thin and scrawny, almost emaciated, with long black hair that shed onto the floor and into the food. She had a sensitive, intelligent face, but there was something about her that irritated me. Perhaps it was because she had a way of whining when she talked, giving her a "me too" attitude that made me feel guilty when I had no reason to be.

She was put into *infarad* with Laurel and me, and from that moment I felt a tension in the air—a nervous itching, like another cockroach crawling along my leg.

"Be nice to her," Esther told us. "She has been in the prison hospital with typhoid . . . she's had a really tough time."

So to please Esther, we helped her make a bed out of some blankets because there wasn't an extra mat, and we arranged our own mats to make more room for her. But I resented having to do it, and I resented her being there.

The next morning, Laurel and I went to Alia's

for Arabic coffee and breakfast. We were eating granola when Suzanne burst in. "You had to sneak out, didn't you?" she cried. "You're over here eating without me. It isn't fair! It isn't fair!" I was shocked. I had never come to Alia's room until I was invited. But Suzanne would go anywhere for food, especially if she didn't pay for it.

If there was tension in *infarad,* there was even more in the rest of the prison. Hanni, the large, masculine-looking guard who hated all the foreigners, began locking us up for the night when it was only midafternoon.

"I hate this," said Laurel. "It's so unfair. Let's see if *Sit* Marie will let us out."

So we stood at the little hatch in the locked door and took turns calling out, *"Iftahi al-bab . . . iftahi al-bab!"* ("Unlock the door!") If *Sit* Marie were on duty, she would hear our shouts, and, to spite Hanni, who was her rival, she would unlock the door and let us out. But if she wasn't on duty, our calls were useless. We would stay locked in for the rest of that day and often part of the next.

When Hanni and *Sit* Marie were on duty together, no one knew what to expect. If *Sit* Marie allowed us to go out into the courtyard to sunbathe, Hanni would be sure to see us and make us come back in.

Both women had worked in Sanayeh for over twenty years and had become almost like prisoners themselves—sleeping and eating there, and being locked in with us at night by the soldiers outside. Getting another job was out of the question for them. They were too poor and un-educated. The prison was their whole existence, and each one was determined to run it her way. Little by little they began to use the prisoners as pawns in their war for power.

The women divided into two groups: those for Hanni and those for *Sit* Marie. Daily the tension grew, as the prisoners whispered in the hallways, "Are you on Hanni's side or *Sit* Marie's?"

One day, Fowzia, an Arab prisoner who favored *Sit* Marie, started the rumor that Hanni had been seen fondling an Egyptian prisoner on the bench outside the foreigners' room the night before.

"Is it true?" I asked Laurel.

"I didn't see anything. If anybody else saw it, they're afraid to say so. But the rumor now is that Fowzia will be murdered—" she lowered her voice "—strangled in her room tonight. The girls who are for Hanni have already thrown all of Fowzia's things outside in the hall."

The next morning Fowzia was gone. Transferred to another prison by the *ra'eb,* who must have believed the murder threats. But the prisoners on Hanni's side felt that she had been shamed and must be avenged. A day or two later, Su'ad, the head of the kitchen crew, came into *infarad.*

"May I borrow your tape recorder?" she asked Laurel in Arabic.

Laurel hesitated, then shrugged. *"N'am,"* she answered. "Yes, of course."

"I couldn't see what harm there was," she told me later. But there was harm. That day when I went to the kitchen to prepare our dinner, none of the kitchen girls was there to haggle with me as they usually did. By lockup that night, Laurel knew why.

"They were in the storage room recording all the rumors they knew about *Sit* Marie," she told me. Laurel threw up her hands and looked at me in desperation. She had wanted no part in what was going on. She had tried hard to remain neutral. Now they had involved her by using her tape.

"They said that *Sit* Marie has been working in cahoots with Samerya," she whispered.

Samerya? I wondered a second, then remembered that she was the queen bee, the madam of room four, where most of the prostitutes were kept.

"They told everything they know about it," Laurel went on. "How Hasum gets the prostitutes' papers signed by the office so they can be released in five days. The way Samerya recruits girls from the short-termers who come in for petty theft. And how some of the short-termers are now working for *Sit* Marie in her home, being hired out as prostitutes. What's worse, I think they have given the tape to one of the soldiers who is taking it to the commandant!"

I knew what Laurel said was probably true. She knew everyone in the prison and was rarely taken in by false rumors.

We watched Hanni and *Sit* Marie closely. Did

we imagine their nervousness, the quick movements of their eyes, as if they each thought they were being followed?

Riots began breaking out in the hallways, led by a black Sudanese girl in room one. Her name was Maufeeda, and she refused to go into her room at night, protesting loudly instead and complaining about mistreatment. One night, the protests turned to screams. We rushed to the door and saw one of the male guards beating Maufeeda with a stick. Things were clearly getting out of hand, but all we dared do was wait and watch, for it was dangerous for the foreigners to take sides.

Early one morning, the word went out, *"Ufatish, ufatish . . ."* the guards warned us. Our rooms were going to be searched. The whole prison was in a stir while the guards helped us hide all the *memnua* items—forbidden things like radios, mirrors, metal containers or glass bottles, cameras, watches, or film. They knew we had these things, and they didn't care. But they realized that they would be in a lot of trouble if any *memnua* items were found in a search.

After the midday meal was served, Hanni and *Sit* Marie rushed through the halls, locking the doors. "The commandant is coming. Quick . . . inside! *Yalla! Yalla!*" But they could not lock up room one, because Maufeeda wasn't there. As they were looking for her, someone called out, "He is here. The commandant has arrived."

The prison became deathly still. We listened for the quick heavy footsteps of the *ra'eb* and his soldiers . . . for the commandant. It was too quiet. I didn't like this. Why had Maufeeda disappeared. What was she up to?

The commandant appeared at the end of the hall, standing stiff and straight as if at attention, one hand across his chest in the front of his uniform, Napoleon-style. Almost as if by a signal, the halls began to echo with the sound of plastic hitting the tile floor. From every room, prisoners were hurling their dishes still filled with food from the midday meal. Food flew through the unlatched windows of every door and splattered on the soldiers and against the walls.

Suddenly Maufeeda and the missing girls from room one were out in the hallway, surrounding the commandant and the *ra'eb*.

Because Hanni and *Sit* Marie had not had time to lock our door, we stood and watched from our end of the hall as Maufeeda began to dance. Her feet touched the tile floor in quick, rhythmic steps. The other girls joined her, swaying to the rhythm. Then Maufeeda began to sing. Her voice rose, loud and clear, in a sad, defiant song that mocked the *ra'eb* and the prison. All the terror, all the tension of the last days erupted in her voice in a strange, tribal chant.

She sang of Su'ad who sold the prison food for profit. Of prisoners who never received the meat they were due. Of only one meal a day. The girls in the hall began to repeat some of her words, chanting in a strange melody that was soon taken up and echoed by all the other prisoners.

Her voice grew louder and rose to a shriek. The *ra'eb* reached out for her, tried to push her into her room, but the harder he pushed her, the angrier she became. The voices of the others rose with hers, screaming, shrieking. Their anger was turning to open hatred.

I felt as though I wanted to run somewhere and get out of sight. There had been other riots—smaller than this—but they had always settled down and died. Today, no one was in control. Not the guards, not Maufeeda, not even the commandant himself.

I could hear his voice, rising above the others, shouting angrily. But no one listened. I saw the *ra'eb* reach out and grab Maufeeda by both shoulders and shake her hard. Her song ended in one last defiant, ear-piercing scream. For a few seconds, the prison was silent. Two guards began to move slowly forward.

"*Fostu le juwa*—go inside," the commandant urged. "I will come tomorrow—*bukra*—tomorrow I will hear your complaints."

No one obeyed. No one moved. The guards reached out and took the women by their arms, struggled with them, pushing them roughly toward the room. Voices rose in angry protest. One guard seized Maufeeda and dragged her toward her room. She screamed frantically and twisted away, clawing at his face with her nails.

Suddenly she wrenched away and picked up a wooden bench and hurled it at him. The guard sidestepped, and the bench fell with a crash to the floor, where it broke in two. He grabbed her again and held her arms twisted behind her back until she cried out in pain.

The *ra'eb* spoke a few words in Arabic, and

some soldiers left and returned with rubber hoses. Again and again they struck the women, raising ugly red welts on their bodies and screams of pain from their throats. I covered my ears to shut out the dull thuds against human flesh.

I wanted to run for my mat and the scanty protection of my little corner. But I was afraid to move—afraid that any commotion would bring the guards to this end of the hall. I watched as Maufeeda staggered into her room, and the guards slammed the door behind her.

The latches were jammed into place, and the padlock thudded against the door. She was locked in for the night, but she wasn't finished. We could hear her voice, rising and falling in a mournful chant that told of her agony. Before long, the other prisoners joined her, drumming a low, monotonous rhythm that lasted far into the night.

CHAPTER

14

The next day the door was opened briefly in the morning by Hanni and *Sit* Marie themselves. They quickly passed the water in, then slammed the door shut. We could do nothing but sit and wait. Would the commandant really return and listen to complaints? Or would the women be punished and then forgotten, as they had been many times in the past? The sun's rays moved slowly across the floor until I knew it was almost noon.

Finally, I heard male voices in the halls. "The commandant is here. He is here." The words moved rapidly from one room to the next, changing dialect and language as they passed down the hall. "Anyone who has a complaint can speak with the commandant privately."

One by one the rooms were unlocked, and a few women stepped forward into a hallway that was filled with guards—the regular ones plus reinforcements from outside the prison.

"Yalla! Yalla!" I could hear Hanni and *Sit* Marie yelling for the women to hurry. But they moved slowly along the hall, most of them hesitant and a little fearful after the previous night's demonstration.

Rahaili wouldn't go at all, and I could understand why. She had been here a long time and knew what things were really like. She knew who cheated and who mistreated, and she knew how they did it. But her two children were being taken care of by Hanni, and Rahaili didn't dare say anything against her. Instead, she was very quiet and stayed close to her room.

When our turn came later in the day, Laurel went forward to speak to the commandant. "You are the one who should see him," we had told her. "You know more about what goes on in the prison than we do."

She was gone only a short time. When she came back, she had surprising news. "Anyone who wants to be transferred to another prison may leave tomorrow," she said. "Lots of the women have decided to go, but I don't know—I keep wondering if they're right. Things could be even worse somewhere else."

Twenty-three prisoners didn't think so. They chose to take their chances somewhere else. Even Rahaili, who had been here so long and had promised Alia that she would stay, decided at last to pack her few things and leave. Who knew the reason why? Rahaili kept her own confidence.

By lunchtime the next day, *Sit* Marie and Hanni began calling out the slow roll call of names.

Laurel and I ran to Alia's room to tell Rahaili good-bye. We watched as Alia handed Rahaili her small bundle of clothes. They embraced, their eyes wet with tears. They were unable to speak because they were both sobbing.

I walked forward with Rahaili when she was called to leave, but Alia remained in the room crying, with Laurel's arms around her.

When we got up front, everyone was standing around, watching the women walk to the army jeeps that waited to take them away. Their belongings were tied in sheets with the four corners pulled together. They looked like war prisoners, or refugees leaving for unknown camps. Fear and uncertainty showed on their faces. There was no laughter. These women had made their choice, and there was no turning back.

I hugged Rahaili good-bye. Tears were hot on my cheeks as I returned to the room where Laurel was still comforting Alia, holding her slight frame and rocking her like a baby.

I cried as I hadn't cried since I entered Sanayeh.

After they were gone, it was like death had visited the prison—it was so bare and lonely. Laurel and I stayed in room six with Alia that night. But I kept remembering Rahaili's remarkable face. I had intended to draw her, and now it was too late.

As a result of the riots, both *Sit* Marie and Hanni were suspended. Su'ad was relieved of her kitchen duties, and other prisoners who were serving long sentences took over. A new regime began, but it was worse than the last.

Now Alia was constantly ostracized. The new girls who took over had always been jealous of her; now they ignored her. Laurel and I were her only friends, which increased the tension, since we were foreigners.

With Rahaili gone, the trustees didn't always unlock the foreigners' rooms. We would wait and wait, and no one would come to let us out. Finally, I began my own war against their Arab implacability.

As soon as I awoke in the morning—about six o'clock—I would put my head through the small, square opening in the door and see who was walking the hall. Then I would begin calling her name.

"Min fadlik, iftahi al-bab." ("Please, open the door.")

A few of the trustees would respond. Others kept me yelling for hours, and some of them ignored me entirely, and we were not unlocked all day.

There were days when the water was short, and the foreigners didn't get any at all. The trustees who took our orders for shopping became more and more irregular. Many days they never came. Other times the food we ordered never appeared. We all worried about this, but Suzanne was the only one who couldn't cope.

One evening during dinner, she accused me of not giving her a fair share. "You've got more beans on your plate than I do," she complained.

I looked at her in surprise, then reached over and scraped some of my dinner onto her plate. Maybe that would shut her up. She devoured it eagerly without a word. It was food that we provided for her because she didn't have any money. But she still felt free to complain.

She was beginning to irritate me more every day. It wasn't just her greediness with food. She had such a whiney voice, and she ate with her mouth open so everyone could see the chewed-up food. She was an American, but she simply wasn't up to my standards. I felt ashamed for her, because she didn't have the sense to feel ashamed for herself.

Finally one day the truck came to take me back to B'abda—not for my trial, but so that I could sign for my lawyer and confirm my story. I sat in the back of the truck, waiting anxiously as it pulled into the courtyard of Ramal, wondering if Dimitri would also be riding into B'abda today.

Suddenly I saw him being led across the yard. In a few seconds he was climbing into the back of the truck. He lifted his face and saw me.

"Marti," he said. "Oh, Marti. . . ."

He sat beside me, leaned close and brushed my lips with his. I leaned my head on his shoulder. So much had happened, I thought. So many misunderstandings. But my feelings for him had never really changed. Even now, in the back of a dirty army truck, bumping along the rutty road to B'abda, he could touch me, and bring back an Easter night in Athens, when we had watched the candles and then the stars together.

We talked briefly of our case. "We have made things so complicated for ourselves," he said. "How stupid I have been, Marti."

I put my hand on his. "It will all be over. Sooner or later this will end," I told him.

We arrived at B'abda and could speak no more. I was put back into one of the underground holding cells to wait my turn. An older woman who had just been arrested was already there. She called herself Madame Chevalier and said she was French and Egyptian, but she spoke English quite well and was anxious to talk.

"Are you in the women's prison?" she asked. "What is it like?" She was full of questions, wanting to know all about the sleeping, eating, and washing arrangements.

I remembered how I had felt when I was in her place and Laurel had come into the cell and talked to me. "Don't worry," I told her. "It's not good at Sanayeh, but we manage. You can ask for me when you come."

"But where will they put me?" She shook her head in obvious distress. "I am not well, you see. My back has been broken and gives me such great pain. And my liver . . . oh, I don't want to burden you. I might as well be dead." She hesitated, then looked at me hopefully. "Could . . . could I stay where you are? Is there room for one small, sad woman?"

What difference would it make? I thought. This woman couldn't be any worse than Suzanne, and we were putting up with her. "We'll work something out," I promised.

A few days later, she arrived and moved into

163

our room. There were five of us in *infarad* now: Laurel and myself, Suzanne, Madame Chevalier, and a short-termer named Sophia. The small room that had seemed just right for Lily, Laurel, and me was now overcrowded and full of bickering. Sitting, lying, or standing with not much more than an arm's length between us, we found that each small annoyance became magnified.

I began joining Laurel in room six for breakfast with Alia, and many nights Laurel would stay there to sleep. Whenever I could, I escaped and went elsewhere to read or write letters—to Alia's room, to the courtyard if it was open, or to some corner of the guards' room, until they caught me and made me leave.

But there was often nowhere else to go. Then I stayed in *infarad,* trying to ignore Suzanne's whining and avoiding Madame Chevalier, who was constantly complaining about her bad back and sick liver. I had problems of my own, but she didn't care. She never seemed to sense how the rest of us felt.

From the very first day, she had demanded our attention, and she had complained about everything. "I can't sleep on one of those little mats," she exclaimed. The commandant was visiting that day—making a short tour of inspection after all the rioting—and she walked right over to him and told him so.

"I have a very bad back. It was severely broken," she said. "I absolutely must have a mattress!" She told him in Arabic, and Laurel translated it for me. We couldn't believe her nerve and laughed to ourselves. But she got her mattress, anyway. The commandant ordered it for her that very day. She put her two suitcases underneath and had a regular bed to sleep on.

Laurel shrugged. "That ought to keep her happy for a while."

"Not that one," Alia told her. And Alia was right. Every time Madame Chevalier—"Chevy"—wanted to leave her bed, she lay there and extended her hand, waiting to be helped up.

"Please, ladies," she would say. "I must not strain my back."

We went along with it for a while, but it began to get tiresome always to be waiting on Chevy. "This is getting pretty old," I whispered to Laurel. "She's too heavy for me to help up."

She nodded. "Do you see how spry she is whenever they bring out the food? She jumps right out of bed with her little bowl and spoon and gets at the head of the line."

Madame Chevalier had decided to eat the prison food, and that was just fine with us. She would fill her bowl in the hall and bring it back to the room to eat her dinner. She had a funny habit of always smelling each bite, holding it close to her nose and sniffing loudly before putting it into her mouth.

We decided to ignore her, but her moans continued. "I'm dying," she would say. "I have nothing to live for. No money. No way to earn any except by smuggling hashish, and I can't do that now."

Laurel and I tried to talk to her, to tell her there were other ways she could earn a living. But she always denied it. "Nothing. I can do nothing," she would insist. "Neither can my husband. We're done. Finished. Oh, my poor, sick husband—my poor liver—my poor back. I really am dying. Don't bother about me. Just consider me dead."

Laurel and I knew that she wasn't telling the truth. Her poor, sick husband was already dead. And we had our doubts about the condition of her back and liver. But it was easier to just let her rave on and try not to listen. Suzanne, however, had no patience with her. "Be still!" she would scream. "I can't stand the sound of your voice!"

Chevy would look right back at her and curse. Then, "Shut up, yourself, you filthy savage!" Soon they would be shouting at each other, screaming insults, each one listing the things the other did to annoy her.

I began to hate our room and everything about it. It had been such a quiet, peaceful place. But now everything was changed. There was nowhere to be alone, no place to be quiet. I was doing most of the cooking and hating that, too. It had been so different when Laurel and I were doing everything together. Some days I felt as dead as Chevy claimed to be.

"Just consider me dead, too!" I finally snapped at her. She looked at me, shocked. But she quieted down for a while.

Early one morning, Laurel motioned for me to follow her into the courtyard. She had just been up front for a visit with Mary Mathias.

When we reached the far wall, she looked all around us to be sure no one could hear what she said. "I'm getting out," she whispered.

"What!" I stared at her in disbelief. At the end of July she had been convicted and sentenced to three years for trafficking. I knew that Mary had been appealing her case, and I had heard how Mary's life had been threatened for doing it. Laurel's case, like Lily's, was different. It clearly involved much more than simple smuggling. Someone was involved at a high government level and didn't want to risk exposure. Everyone—Iraqis, Jordanians, Palestinians, Lebanese, and even Americans—was interested in Laurel's case, and Mary received eight to ten inquiries about it each week.

I wondered how Mary had managed to get her release. As far as I knew, only one prisoner had ever been released from Sanayeh before the usual eighteen months—and that was because she was dying.

"No one can know about this," Laurel warned me. "But Mary has told me to get ready. The president himself will give me a special amnesty, and I'll have to get out of the country at once."

I cried tears of joy for Laurel and tried to hide my own sorrow. She began spending most of her evenings with Alia because of our overcrowded room, and so she could prepare to leave. I began to see what life in Sanayeh was going to be like without her. I would be left holding the bag. I would have to be the one to keep things calm and organized. And I would have to do it all by myself. No one else in our room cared. I thought briefly of moving back into room seven, but I put it quickly out of my mind. The girls in there didn't even like me.

One night a guard appeared at our door. "Workmen will be here tomorrow," she told Laurel. "Clear this room out after you are unlocked, so they will have room to work."

Early the next morning, we learned what was going on: the Arabs needed more room. One week during the summer there had been 103 women in the prison—almost double the capacity, and some of the Arab prisoners had had to sleep in the kitchen and in the bathrooms.

So they had decided to knock a big hole in the wall of *infarad,* combining it with room six to form a larger room for the Arabs. In room seven, the foreigners' room, the bathroom and the coffin walls would be knocked down, making one big room where all the foreigners would stay. A new bathroom would be added at the end. Finally, the tree in the courtyard would be taken down, and a brand new room for the Arabs would be built on the other side of the hall from us, using some of the courtyard area.

By noon, workmen holding big sledgehammers were pounding on the wall between *infarad* and room six. Each bang of the hammers seemed to destroy any privacy or peace we had known. *Infarad* would soon be gone, I thought sadly. Sanayeh had never seemed so miserable.

Plaster flew everywhere, dropping on my mat and falling into my boxes. Smash! A vase of flowers that the Paeths had given me fell to the floor. Everything was being destroyed in a few short hours. I ran out to the courtyard, coughing up the fine, choking dust that filled the prison air, and breathing in the fresh, clean air of late October.

By three o'clock, a huge hole had been knocked out of the wall between the two rooms. The workmen stood back and inspected it, then left without a word, leaving their tools and huge chunks of fallen plaster littering the floor. They would be back tomorrow, but how would we sleep in this mess tonight?

We got boxes from the storage room and loaded them up with as much of the debris as we could scrape together. Then we brought in buckets of water and tried to mop up the fine, powdery dust from the floor.

When a new girl, Virginia, arrived late in the afternoon, it seemed to me to be the final indignation in an already bad day. I said I was too tired to organize new sleeping arrangements and escaped to Alia's room instead, letting the others worry about it for a change.

When I returned, my mat had been pushed into a dark corner away from the window, where there was little or no fresh air to even stir the dust which still filled the room.

The next day, the workmen began tearing down the bathroom wall in the foreigners' *loo*. Again plaster flew, crumbling into the dust that choked the prison. It was Saturday, visiting day, and I was grateful for the time I was allowed to spend up front.

The Paeths brought friends—David and Maxine King, who were missionaries in Beirut. I talked to them eagerly, taking as much time as I could, putting off my return to the shambles of our room.

When I did return, I saw the girls from room seven sitting out in the hall, their clothes and boxes crowded close beside them. Their room was so torn up they couldn't possibly sleep in it for the night.

I had never felt close to those girls, but right now they looked like I felt. We had so little that belonged to us at Sanayeh—our clothes, our precious cardboard boxes, our little supplies of food and books, and the piece of floor we slept on. Their faces showed that they had lost much of that, and feared losing more.

There was nothing to do but move them in with us. What was left of *infarad* was a mass of crowded bodies and boxes all trying to fit into a cramped space. We had to put all our food together and share it by candlelight, then spread our mats out, overlapping, side by side on the floor and try to sleep.

The next days went by in much the same way, with the foreigners shifting from room to room as the workmen tore down more walls, then began rebuilding. We began to cough from the plaster dust as the powdery air filled our lungs— deep, rattling coughs that only became worse as we took in great breaths of the unclean air. There was no privacy at all, for the workmen were everywhere—and appeared at unexpected moments. The steady thudding of hammers and the harsh shouting of the workmen's voices began to make our heads pound.

I spent as much time as possible with Alia and Laurel in room six, for Laurel would be leaving any day now, and we didn't even know if we would have enough warning to say good-bye. "I'll write you, Marti," she promised. "And I'll try to send you things."

I wanted to tell her it wouldn't be the same. I would be so lonely here without her. But I smiled and nodded, for Laurel was getting out, and nothing should be allowed to ruin that.

She left at noon on the last day of October. As she was getting ready to leave, she gave me a little book to keep. "This is for you, Marti. It's something Esther gave me." I looked at the title: *Love in the Words and Life of Jesus.* I treasured it because it was a gift from Laurel. But I was in no mood for reading.

I walked to the door with her a few moments later. Mary Mathias was there waiting. They left together, walking out of the prison to freedom. Laurel turned to wave, and then she was gone.

Suddenly, I didn't know what to do or where to go. I couldn't bear the thought of returning to *infarad* just then and facing the problems of Suzanne and Madame Chevalier. I didn't really have a friend to talk to now, except Alia. But I couldn't speak Arabic, and she spoke very little English.

Alia asked me to move into room six with her, but I knew I couldn't adjust to living there all the time. The Arab schedule meant being in bed by ten o'clock and knitting most of the day. The women in there never seemed to read or write, and of course they spoke Arabic all the time. I would be lost in there, even with Alia's kindness.

But I was lost, anyway. I couldn't go to room seven, and my own room was a miserable succession of fights between Suzanne and Chevy. My only hope now was the trial. It was only a few days away. The judge had to exonerate me. He just had to. I couldn't stand Sanayeh any longer.

CHAPTER

15

November 2 came at last. I sat in the public courtroom at B'abda, waiting with the other defendants until my case was called. I was excited and nervous and afraid. I had wanted to look my best; but I knew I didn't. My face was terrible—red and pimply. It made me look like I had some kind of disease. And I was so overweight that my clothes didn't fit, making me look swollen and puffy.

At least I knew that I looked clean, which was more than I could say for Dimitri or Alexandrou. The hair on Dimitri's shaven skull was growing out in short, prickly stubs. He was terribly thin and so nervous that his hands shook when he tried to smoke the cigarettes I had brought him. He wore that same brown pin-striped suit, and it was badly wrinkled and covered with stains. I was irritated with him, because he had said something about my face.

"How dare you!" I snapped. "You have no right to say anything about the way I look. It's because of you that I look this way!"

Alexandrou had gained weight and had a thick look about him that wasn't healthy. I didn't like him any better than before and tried to avoid looking at him.

The front portion of the courtroom was divided, with all the defendants sitting on one side facing the representatives from their embassies on the other. I could see Bob Paeth and the man from the American Embassy sitting across from me in the second row.

In the front of the room on an elevated platform sat the three judges, one officially called the president or presiding judge, and two counselors. These three men alone would decide if we were innocent or guilty. Our fate was held in their hands, for there was no jury.

Our assorted attorneys, dressed in long black robes, sat at a table just below the judges. Dimitri had fired his old attorney when he learned about the blackmailing incident and had hired a new one—the first one, I thought, who looked the least bit dignified or trustworthy. Mary Mathias was there, sitting behind a stack of papers and files, the only woman among many men.

A number of spectators, probably relatives of those being tried that day, sat out in the main part of the courtroom.

My face began to itch, and I longed to reach up and scratch it, but I couldn't afford to make it look any worse than it did. I clenched my hands in my lap instead and concentrated on watching the judges as they listened to the cases that preceded ours.

Two of them looked so tired and bored that I was sure they weren't listening. Their eyelids were nearly closed. It was impossible to tell if they were studying the papers on the table before them or dozing. The other one, who Mary told me later was Judge Brady, the president, had a prominent nose and large angular face. He was awake and listening. He was the only one who seemed perceptive enough to think beyond the magistrate's report. I would look at him when I testified, I decided. I didn't want this thing rubber-stamped again.

I began to go over the details of our case in my mind, rehearsing what it was I was supposed to say. This time I couldn't afford to make any mistakes. I was going to take time to think before I spoke.

Finally, our case was called. Dimitri, Alexandrou, and I stood up and went before the judges. Dimitri was asked to tell his story first; then his attorney began asking questions. Each question had to be repeated three times. First, Dimitri's attorney would tell the judge in Arabic what he wished to ask. The judge would repeat it out loud, and only then would the interpreter translate it into English to be answered.

I waited nervously for the question that mattered most to me—the one I dreaded the most. At last the judge asked, "Did your fiancée, Miss Marti Sinclair, know that the hashish was in her suitcase?"

175

I held my breath. Would he tell them the truth? So much depended on Dimitri's answer.

"No," I heard him say. "She knew nothing at all."

"Why are you denying her knowledge now, when your original statement said that she was implicated?"

"The customs officers misunderstood," Dimitri claimed. His voice was calm and steady. "There was no interpreter at that time to help me. What I am telling you now is the truth."

He lied with such ease, I thought. But then, so did I. I watched the judge carefully as Dimitri spoke. What was he thinking? There was no way I could get past the stern face—no way to know what was going on inside his head.

It was my turn to testify. I stood there before the three men and told them my version of what had happened. When I finished, I realized that my hands were pressed into tight fists, with my thumbs enclosed inside. I opened them slowly, determined to look relaxed. My fingers felt tight and swollen.

Mary addressed the president and her words were repeated by the judge, then translated into English for me. "Marti, were there any mistakes in the registration of your statements in front of the examining magistrate?"

"Yes," I replied. Mary and I had already rehearsed what I would say. Because my statements had been made in front of only one official, with no witnesses present, I would claim that my testimony had been inaccurately translated.

"The record states that I said that Dimitri

didn't leave the room we slept in that night in Yammoune. I never said that. What I said was that I didn't know whether he left the room or not. I was asleep, and I don't know what he did."

I took a deep breath. Was the judge listening to me? Evidently he was, for he said something to the interpreter. "Is there anything else?" he wanted to know.

"Just one more thing. We went to Yammoune as sightseers. That is all I know. If any arrangements had to be made for us to get there, they were made without my knowledge. I did not know the area had been cordoned off. I was only in Beirut to see the sights, not to smuggle hashish."

I looked up at Judge Brady as the translator repeated my words in Arabic. Was his face softening a little? I couldn't tell.

Mary pulled some telegrams and letters from her files and showed them to Brady and the other judges. Brady handed them to the translator. "Do you know these people?" he asked me.

I nodded. "Yes, I do. Una Sinclair is my mother. Reverend Garcia is the chairman of the board of directors of the counseling center I administer. John Moreno is the chief of police in the community our counseling center serves."

Mary took the papers and read them out loud in Arabic, then handed them to the interpreter, who read them again in English.

"Martha Sinclair is a young woman of character and ideals who, though very young, has been dedicated to working with young people and their problems. Please help her, and return her to us. This girl is not a criminal. . . ."

Finally, the statement from Reverend Garcia was presented. "It is incongruent in our minds how Martha, who has put all her energies into our program—which has as a high priority the drug problem and its consequences—and who is financially set, could be connected in any way with the trafficking of drugs. It is against our agency and her life-style itself. . . ."

I looked down at the floor. These people had all believed in me enough to write letters like that, and I hadn't even told them the truth. What would they think of me if they knew? But they didn't have to know. If I could just convince these three men that I was innocent, I would be free to go home, and no one need ever know.

I thought about the prison—of Suzanne and Madame Chevalier, of the riots, the food, and the filth. I couldn't go back to that place. I would bluff this thing out to the finish. I raised my head and looked squarely at the judges. *I'm innocent. Look at me, everybody! I'm innocent. Can't you see that Dimitri is responsible?*

Alexandrou was giving his testimony, once again denying everything, claiming complete innocence as he had done before. It didn't matter. My testimony and Dimitri's had agreed in every detail. We had not slipped up once. Somehow I felt that, this time, we were winning.

But Dimitri's attorney seemed to be pressing for something more. I didn't know what he was saying, but I watched Mary as she rustled the papers in front of her. Her eyes began blinking, as they always did when she was upset. Suddenly her face flushed. She stood up and began speaking loudly in Arabic. Her voice was angry, vehement.

What could have gone wrong? I looked frantically from one face to the other, but they were all speaking rapidly in Arabic, and there wasn't a single word I could understand. I didn't know what to do. They might be deciding something that would affect the rest of my life, yet I seemed no more important to these officials than the fly that was buzzing around my head.

The judges conferred briefly. Brady spoke with Mary, and I recognized one word. *"La."* And I knew it meant "No." Then he announced something to the entire courtroom. Again I heard words that I understood. December 14, 1974. What was going to happen on that date?

When it was over, Mary came toward me. "The case has been postponed," she said. "I don't know how long it will drag on now." She paused and shot Dimitri a withering look. "Dimitri's attorney has asked that he be put in Asforiya, the local mental hospital, to determine if his use of drugs has impaired his ability to think properly. If the doctor says that this has happened, then the court will rule that he is not responsible, and he will go free. But it may take months."

"But, Mary," I protested, "what does that have to do with me? Can't they give me a decision now?"

She shook her head. "I have already asked the judge to disassociate your case from the other two and make an independent judgment. He refused. You will have to wait at least until December 14, when the doctors will report. If all goes well, we will make our final pleas on that day, and the case will be given to the judges for a verdict. If not, I just don't know what will happen.''

''Oh, Mary!'' I had no more words. I was too close to tears. A month and a half more—at least. I didn't see how I could stand that. But I wasn't being given any choice. Somehow I would have to find a way to live through the next six weeks.

On the way back to Sanayeh in the back of the truck, I kept telling myself that it was only for six more weeks. But a nagging question kept raising its head like a serpent in my mind—what if it were more than six weeks? What then?

The next days were nightmares. I cleaned frantically, scrubbing viciously everything in sight. I couldn't seem to stop working, sorting my boxes, rearranging, keeping busy—busy—busy. I hated my room and everyone in it. I didn't want to talk about the trial, or the postponement, or anything at all. I only wanted to be left alone so I could find something else to work at. At night I fell exhausted onto my mat, wishing that I could sleep and sleep and not wake up until this nightmare were over.

We couldn't go out into the courtyard because of the construction, and I began to think that perhaps the condition of my face was due to lack of sun. It seemed worse each day, swollen and red and covered with large, itchy pimples. I couldn't seem to keep my hands off of them and began to pick at my face daily. The pimples developed into large painful boils, new ones appearing each day. And still I picked at them nervously, pressing against the sides of the large round lumps, trying to get them to burst and release the pus.

Esther wrote me a letter saying that if I could only relax and accept the fact that I was in prison, my poor face might clear up. I was furious. How dare she even hint that I might not have complete control of myself? Didn't she know that I was administrator to a counseling center? I was the most "together" person I knew!

One day as I was getting supplies from the storeroom, I glanced in the large mirror the guards kept there. I was horrified at the reflection I saw, but I couldn't seem to turn away. I stared for a long time at the angry red welts that covered most of my face. Some of them were open and oozing with blood and white pus. I was so ugly! The red knots on my face hid everything else. How could anyone see the person behind that gnarled mass I called a face?

I dropped the supplies I had gathered and ran back to *infarad*, collecting the things I needed for a steam facial. Then I went into the kitchen and heated water. I lowered my head close to the sink and put a towel over it, closing in the steam. The hot, wet air seeped into the open sores on my face, stinging my skin until my eyes watered. But I continued until the water cooled, and then I heated some more.

After a while, I stood up and looked out the little opening in the barbed wire that covered the window above the sink. My mind tried to escape from the body that was locked in this prison and roam free, outside—down Sanayeh Street and east toward the airport. But my burning face kept bringing me back, back inside the barbed wire, back to the sores on my face, back to the anger raging inside me. I began to sob uncontrollably, my body shaking with the pain that I felt within.

"Marti? Is that you?"

It was a crisp but concerned British voice. Someone was behind me. I kept my head turned away and hid my face. "I don't want anyone to see me looking like this. Get out of here . . . leave me alone!"

"What's wrong, Marti? Can I help you?"

It was Anne—one of the girls from room seven. She had always looked so American to me, with her shoulder-length blonde hair and natural good looks—like someone on the cover of *Glamour* or *Mademoiselle*. Like someone from home.

She came over and put her hand on my shoulder until I stopped crying. Slowly, a little at a time, I managed to tell her everything—how much I hated Suzanne and how much Madame Chevalier irritated me. How I missed Laurel, and what had happened at the trial. There wasn't any need for me to talk about my face. Its condition was obvious enough.

"Look, Marti, why don't you move into room seven with us? Most of the old girls are gone now, and two more are leaving soon. Penny and I are trying to make things different in there.

You're welcome to move in with us.''

I looked at her in surprise. I had been sure that the girls in room seven didn't like me. Maybe Anne was right. Maybe things in there had changed. The next day I gathered my things together and placed my mat in room seven near Anne and her friend Penny. Above me was a small window that let in a little fresh air. I brought Lily's table and put it next to my mat on one side, and my boxes on the other. The other two girls in the room would be leaving soon, giving us a little more room.

That night, Anne, Penny, a very pregnant Aiya, and I ate dinner together, then exchanged stories. I told of my meeting with Dimitri, of our life together in London, and our trip to Beirut. But I didn't tell them the truth about my guilt.

Anne lit another cigarette and started her story. "I lived in Rome with my boyfriend, Nicole, and we flew to Beirut for a romantic vacation. . . ."

She paused while Penny shook her short auburn hair, stretched her long, thin legs, and continued the conversation with her story. "I, too, lived in Rome and flew to Beirut to meet *my* lover . . . Nicole!"

Anne interrupted. "Penny and I have a lot in common. When Nicole had us both calmed down, he convinced us to help him take some hash back to Rome. That's how we landed here in Sanayeh."

A little later, someone brought out the hash. This time I took it gladly and welcomed the light, airy feeling it gave me. A few puffs, and my mind was freed from the walls that surrounded me. I drifted in space, floating out far beyond the prison. I hung suspended above Beirut. . . . I was home in San Francisco.

During the next days I learned to live regularly like that, with my mind outside the prison walls, dreaming about what was happening at home or about what might happen in the trouble-free future of my imagination. At the end of each dream, I abruptly returned to the same whitewashed walls. But there was always another cigarette—and another.

I wished there were enough to make me stop feeling entirely, for the rooms were becoming cold and clammy as the season turned to winter. Some days it was too cold to bathe at all. We put newspapers on the floor under our mats to help soak up the moisture that collected and to protect us from the cold. It was Penny's idea. "If newspapers keep tramps warm," she said, "maybe they'll keep the cold off of us, too."

Days passed when I seemed to do nothing at all. No reading or writing, no yoga, no art. I just sat around feeling fat and pimply and miserable. The rains came and brought dreary days, wet and colder than ever. Only the evening candlelight and the now pleasant smell of hashish kept me from breaking under the uncertainty that lay ahead.

Often in the evening, after we were locked up for the night, one of the girls would dance the erotic Arabic belly dance to a tape of Arabic music. Her hips would move in a slow, rolling motion as her hands accentuated the beat.

Penny joined in the fun, but Anne and I sat and watched. I felt calm and relaxed from the hashish, but still fearful and filled with guilt for using it. There seemed to be a pendulum inside of me that was out of balance. Why couldn't I handle things better than this? There had to be some other way—but what?

The dark days of November moved forward, and I felt myself growing colder and my mind growing darker. I was still an outsider—alone— and I was beginning to wonder how long I could live this way.

CHAPTER

16

The dark, rainy days of winter reflected my gloomy mood. When the temperature dropped, the boils and pimples on my face seemed to multiply. Some days I would steam my face and apply egg whites. Then a few of the bumps seemed to disappear. But I would always wake up the next morning to find that they had promptly been replaced with more.

I became obsessed with my face, picking at it, steaming it, giving myself egg-white facials, and finally pulling the covers over my head at night and wishing that I could die.

Because of the reconstruction, we were not allowed to go outside into the courtyard during the whole month of November. How I craved sunshine and fresh air when I couldn't have them! How I craved a little space, away from the others. I especially needed to get away from Chevy, who moved in with us one day and began her old routine: "My poor liver . . . my poor back!"

There was no heating system in Sanayeh, and the floors and walls were cold and damp. Water seeped up through the cracks in the floor; rain dripped down through the holes in the ceiling and blew in through the single window that was still uncovered due to the reconstruction work. We piled more and more newspapers between our mats and the floor, trying desperately to keep our bedding dry. But there weren't enough papers in all of Beirut to soak up the moisture that collected in that prison. As soon as the papers were wet, they stayed that way, for it was impossible for the water to evaporate. So we finally gave up and slept at night with moisture seeping through to our skins. Our mats and pillows were wet every morning, and we couldn't even go outside to try to dry them out.

Since we weren't allowed outside even to hang out our laundry, the halls were soon filled with dripping clothes and bedding, adding to the overall dampness and misery.

There was a big clothes box in the hallway, and as girls were released from Sanayeh they left behind unwanted garments. In desperation we rummaged through it, searching indiscriminately for anything that might fit, trying to layer ourselves against the penetrating chill of the night.

Alia made me a pair of warm gloves, and the Paeths brought extra sweaters and blankets. Typical nightwear for me was thermal underwear beneath my flannel nightgown, a heavy sweater, socks, mittens, and a woolen ski cap. Anne said that I looked like someone ready to go on an Arctic expedition. I would zip myself into the sleeping bag that Laurel had left for me, then try not to move all night for fear of knocking off the blankets I had piled on top.

Often at night the cold would awaken us, and we would lie on our wet mats, shivering, longing to be anywhere, even dead, as long as it was far away from the cold walls of Sanayeh.

Quite suddenly one cold night, Aiya left to have her baby. They immediately put a short-termer in the room to fill her space. She wasn't used to prison life. Like most of the rest of us, she just wasn't prepared to be this miserable.

"It's so cold," she moaned one frigid night. "Won't someone g-give me a b-blanket? Please . . . someone . . . I'm f-freezing."

"We're all cold," Chevy snapped back. "We don't have extra blankets in here." The girl was silent for a few minutes, and then I heard her whimpering again.

"Please. I can't stand this. Oh, someone help me!"

I couldn't stand it any longer, either. I was cold, too, but I wanted them all to shut up and let me get some sleep. Shivering and feeling completely uncharitable, I got out of my snug cocoon and begrudgingly threw her one of my blankets.

"Thank you," she murmured. "I don't know how to thank you."

I didn't bother to answer her. I didn't want

her thanks, just some peace and quiet. I wanted everybody to leave me alone.

In the mornings, as our breaths hit the frosty air, the room turned foggy white. When it wasn't raining outside, the sun sometimes managed to break through and shine upon the courtyard. But we still weren't allowed to go outside.

Our hands were often too cold to do the busy work—the "stiggle"—that had always occupied part of our time. Even letter writing became more of a chore than a pleasure, for our cold fingers ached too much to push a pen across the paper. Eventually, no one wanted to get out of bed at all, and apathy and boredom filled our days.

When we started getting hot water only once a week, most of the girls stopped their daily bathing routines, for the cold water was icy. Even a sponge bath was torture. When hot water did come, it seemed to me like ecstasy to sit in the plastic tub and pour steaming dippers of it over my chilled flesh. My stomach would start to uncramp, my muscles would unknot, and I would start to feel like a person again. But it was a temporary pleasure.

"Hey, Marti . . . get out! I want my turn while the water is still warm." The call would always come too soon, and I would get out, losing all the warmth and relaxation as the cold air hit my skin with the sting of an icy slap.

One afternoon, I received a letter from my sister that ended, ". . . remember that fellow you gave the funny nickname to in college? Well, I had a surprise visit from him last week, and 'G' says hello."

Momentarily I came out of my listlessness. My sister had talked to G. He must know what had happened to me by now. Would he write? Oh, how I longed for him to put words on paper and send them to me.

Anne was cuddled deep into her blankets. "Hey, Marti," she called. "You must have heard from somebody special."

I shook my head. "Not really . . . but my sister had a visit from G."

"Who's this G, and why haven't we heard about him before?" she demanded.

"G is just a nickname I gave him when we were in college. We saw a lot of each other, and I really cared about him. But he was the elusive type—you know what I mean—no strings, no commitments. I saw him briefly just before I left for Europe. Who knows . . . if he had said the right words, I might never have kept my appointment with Dimitri. . . ."

My voice trailed off as I remembered how I had dreamed of a life with G. But it hadn't happened. I was beginning, I thought, to have a succession of things in my life that didn't quite work out.

To escape the darkness of our room, I would often go into the nurse's office and try to catch a fleeting ray of the sunlight that came through her larger window. "Come here, Mona," I would beg. "Come and look at my poor face."

She would search through her drawers and

hand me some medicine. One day I complained so much that she handed me some tranquilizers, too. I swallowed them without a qualm, and they did seem to give me a short relief from the dreariness of my surroundings and the constant new worry that was plaguing me these days.

I hadn't had a period since my arrest. A good five months. I began to imagine that my extra weight was all centered in my stomach. Mornings found me tired and often nauseated. I couldn't be pregnant. I wouldn't be! "O God, don't let it happen!"

The crying of an infant was our only warning that Aiya was back from the prison hospital with her newborn son, Andre. There was no time to get a shelf built for their few belongings. There was no bedding for the baby, not enough blankets to keep him warm. Aiya tried to nurse him, holding him close to her own body to keep away the chill. But he cried constantly—painfully sad little wails. He was cold, and he was hungry, for Aiya did not have enough milk.

We felt so sorry. All of us did. But his constant fretting, day and night, strained our already tense nerves and added weight to the self-pity that was growing among us. Sanayeh was no place for us, much less for a baby. "O God," I cried again. "Don't let it happen to me!"

One day, the dreariness of the cold, dark days was broken by Anne calling out that I had a visitor. "Marti, Dimitri's brother is here!"

I gave my hair a hasty swipe with a brush, then glanced in my little hand mirror to see how I looked. I was appalled. Janis hadn't seen me since Athens, and I didn't want to face him looking like this. But I longed for word from Dimitri, and Janis seemed to be my only reliable contact for now.

"Marti, you look great! You don't even look like you have been in prison," Janis exclaimed.

What a lie! There was nothing to do but ignore it and talk of other things. "How is Dimitri?" I asked.

"Pretty low, I'm afraid. A British fellow died the other day, and all the foreigners took it hard, especially Dimitri."

I could empathize with that. Imagine how I would feel if Laurel or Anne or Penny died here at Sanayeh!

Janis hesitated, as if trying to decide whether or not to tell me something. Suddenly he began speaking, saying it all quickly, in a single breath. "Marti, Dimitri wants me to go to Yammoune—to the same family—and try to get enough hashish this time to pay for a good attorney."

I caught my breath. "Oh, Janis, no! They set us up . . . I'm sure they did. The customs men were waiting for me at the airport. It wasn't even a professional job, with the glue still wet like it was. Mary Mathias told me it was amateur all the way. Listen, Janis, you can't go. You'll end up just like the rest of us."

How could Dimitri have suggested such a thing to his brother? Wouldn't he ever learn? I still dreamed of our life together after prison—but not this way. There could be no future for us if I had to live with the constant fear of Dimitri trying to arrange a deal whenever he needed cash.

"Dimitri is acting like a king up there in the hospital," Janis confided. "He's furious because he thinks they're going to say he's not an addict after all. That means he won't get the insanity report he's been hoping for. Marti, you've got to try to straighten him out. He's threatening to slit his throat if he has to stay in prison."

I felt a chill that had nothing to do with the cold air of the prison. I was beginning to wonder if I knew Dimitri anymore . . . or if I had ever really known him at all.

"Janis, I want to help, but I don't know what I can do from here." I spoke the next words in almost a whisper. "I don't even know if Dimitri will listen to me anymore."

Janis left. I could tell he was disappointed in me. But what could I do? Dimitri might as well be a million miles away for all the communication that existed between us.

The days droned on. I was too depressed to write long letters, too nervous to read, too cold to exercise or concentrate on yoga. They were dark days inside and out, filled with cold despair and little else. "Oh, God, how long can I go on like this? Answer me, God! How long?"

The uncertainty of what might happen etched away at my shattered nerves, but the worst thing to bear was the dreadful, purposeless monotony.

My day started at seven in the morning. I would crawl out of bed and call out to the

guards. If I was lucky, I would get our door unlocked. Then I would have my breakfast, straight-
en out our door rag, have tea, write a letter or
start a cassette tape to send home, rewash the
greasy dishes that Suzanne hadn't washed correctly the night before, and reorganize the cupboards I had organized myself just the day
before. I didn't try to draw. I couldn't seem to
get in the mood for anything that creative.

In the afternoon I would eat again, clean some
more, kill a few cockroaches, then start dinner
while I still had access to the kitchen. Hanni was
back on duty, and her favorite sport was to drive
us away from the kitchen, screaming words in
her harsh, doglike voice that were, to her, ob-
scenities: *"Sharmoota! Americani! Aginabeya!"*
("Prostitute! American! Foreigner!") I was terrified of her and tried to keep out of her way, for
she was big and strong and had a reputation for
hitting the Arab prisoners.

We were locked up at four-thirty every evening and tried to stretch dinner out to fill up the
long, empty evenings. I would do some more rearranging and give my grocery order to one of
the kitchen girls through the window. After Lily
and Laurel left, I had to begin ordering my own
food. What the kitchen girls couldn't bring, I
tried to get through Esther. I tried not to think
back to the days when I hadn't been interested
in ordering food at all, because I had thought I
wasn't going to be here to eat it.

In the evenings after dinner, I would write in
my diary, talk with the girls, and be in bed by
ten. I knew they thought I was bossy, but as long

194

as I was able to be in charge—to manage things and take control of my own surroundings, there seemed to be some sort of order in my life. No purpose, but some sort of order. I badly needed this to survive.

But there was one thing that I never could seem to control. The short-term girl was released, and Suzanne moved in to take her place. Suzanne was with me again, and it was as if I had never escaped from her.

How I hated her! She did nothing the way I thought she should. When our weekly hot water came in, we would all force ourselves to get up and wash our bedding and clothes. Suzanne didn't care much about bathing, and she never managed to get her clothes clean. She didn't even try—just dipped them in the water and wrung them out. The Arab women pointed to her dirty laundry hanging on the line in the hallway and made crude comments about Americans. That embarrassed me—but not Suzanne.

She whined constantly, even more than poor little Andre, and she complained that we gave her too much work and too little food. The rare times she did offer to cook or help with the work, someone, usually me, had to clean up after her. She had the ability to wash dishes with soap and still leave grease all over the plates.

I was growing increasingly irritable with everyone, for not one of the girls was working as hard as I was. But it seemed that most of my anger centered on one object, one scapegoat: Suzanne.

Just looking at her across the room was

enough to drive me mad. I hated her appearance, the sound of her voice, the way she blew her nose. I detested her when she ate, chewing hungrily, greedily. It turned my stomach to see her long black hairs around the room. She didn't even know how to tuck the sheets around her mat to make her bed. She just threw them down and lay on them the way they fell. I always smiled to myself when I heard Chevy call her "filthy savage!" for I knew it was true, and I had been thinking the same thing myself. But when Chevy said it, Suzanne could scream at her instead of me.

In desperation, I tried to show her how to do things the right way. I explained until I was sick of explaining. I even took her with me to the kitchen. When I thought her very presence would drive me completely mad, she came to me crying, "I'm pregnant . . . what should I do?"

"Try growing up!" I snapped. "I'm not your mother. I can barely take care of myself, and I'm sick to death of you. Do you hear me? Sick!"

Not only did she hear me, but so did everybody else. When I had calmed down, Anne came to me. "Marti, don't you think we'd better try to straighten things out between you and Suzanne?"

I was shocked. It was Suzanne's fault that Anne was talking to me like that. Suzanne was making my own friends turn against me. "What's to straighten out?" I demanded. "She hardly ever does any work around here, and what little she does has to be done over by me!"

Suzanne began to whine in her nauseating voice. "But, Marti, I just don't understand you.

196

You're always mad at me—telling me to do more work when I'm already working hard."

"You're not!" I yelled. "Nobody works hard around here but me."

I didn't speak to any of them for the rest of the evening. They were unappreciative clods. Every one of them. That night I wrote in my diary: "Beyond this darkness, there must be a brighter day." There must be, I told myself. It can't be like this forever.

But the dark days stayed with me. Nothing was resolved or changed. Time went on as before, dragging slowly, monotonously, into the deep winter.

By Thanksgiving Day, the reconstruction was finally finished. I determined to force myself to enjoy the day, celebrating our new bathroom and the dinner that the Paeths supplied. When Bob and Jessie delivered the turkey and trimmings, I took the responsibility of cooking and organizing our little feast. The others thought I wanted to do it, but I did it because I had to. I didn't see anyone else stepping in to take my place.

Even on Thanksgiving, my hostility toward Suzanne grew. Every little thing she did annoyed me. When she opened her mouth, I wanted to scream, "Shut up! Won't you just shut up?" even before I heard her voice. I was going to have to do something about her soon. She was making me sick.

That night after I had cleaned up the last of our dinner, I sat down quietly to think. My own feelings were beginning to frighten me. I felt myself slipping out of control. So I did what we used to do at The Bridge. I wrote out a contract with myself:

1. I'll stop being so critical of Suzanne.
2. I'll treat her with the same respect that I give the other girls.
3. Before I speak or react to her, I'll count to ten.

I felt sure I could handle this thing now. I had handled contracts successfully before. My own will had carried me through. Besides, it was foolish to allow one person to make my life miserable. I would get the best of Suzanne yet.

For the next few weeks, I tried hard not to let my hatred show. I didn't like her any better. I didn't even want to like her. But no one could blame me now for her hurt feelings and complaints.

As soon as I thought that I had control of the situation with Suzanne, we began to have to deal daily with what we called "pp" or prison pettiness. Madame Chevalier was a past master at this sort of thing and seemed to take great pleasure in starting little arguments. She played devil's advocate, working one girl against another, delivering half-true messages, passing along bits of gossip, and generally upsetting Arabs, foreigners, and guards alike.

We were all becoming unified in our dislike of this meddlesome woman, and the Arab girls started calling her the "crazy lady." Unexpectedly, a bit of news came that was cause for celebration, even in those dreary days. Chevy was being transferred to another prison.

While she cried, the whole prison, guards and inmates alike, rejoiced together. "Oh, what shall I do?" she sobbed when she left. "My poor back. My liver. When I leave here, I shall die. I am already dead. Just consider me dead." We nodded in agreement. That's just the way we would consider her.

When December came, we were finally allowed to go out into the courtyard again. I immediately felt so much better that I began to believe my health—mental and physical—depended on my getting outside in the sun. The temperature in the courtyard was at least twenty degrees warmer than our room, and I sat there whenever they allowed me to, trying desperately to soak up enough warmth to clear my face before I saw Dimitri on the fourteenth.

But the guards were capricious, and we could never count on their moods. They began refusing to unlock us at all, sometimes keeping us in our rooms all day in solitary confinement.

"A'alama?" I demanded. "Why? What have we done to deserve this? *Kull-yaum!* Every day! You must unlock the door every day."

But the guards watched me curiously as I ranted, then only shrugged and walked away, doing exactly as they pleased—and when it pleased them.

One morning, I grew hysterical at the thought of another day of total confinement. "Open up!

Open up!" I screamed. *"Iftahi al-bab!* I can't breathe in here any longer. Let me out! Let me out!"

I made such a racket that the *ra'eb,* who directed the prison, came to find the source of all the commotion.

"Shu bike?" he demanded. "What's wrong with you?" He didn't give me a chance to explain. "You shut up!" he said. "Shut up, or I'll transfer you to another prison."

His tone alarmed me. I lowered my voice and pleaded softly, "Please unlock the door and let me out. Just for a few minutes. . . ."

"Shut up, I said! I'm going now to get transfer papers. You can join your friend, Madame Chevalier."

As he started toward the office, Alia stopped him and spoke rapidly in Arabic, convincing him to let me stay. I shivered now more from fear than from the cold. He had really meant what he said. What would have happened to me if it wasn't for Alia?

We were locked up as punishment for the next two days. I didn't say a word of complaint, even though my face was worse than it had ever been.

December 14 finally arrived. I woke up early to prepare for my court appearance. Trying to relax, I did yoga, then got unlocked to go put on my makeup. Oh, my poor face! I could hardly bear to look in the mirror. My red dress seemed to make the spots look even worse, but I didn't have anything else that was appropriate to wear.

The truck arrived but was too crowded for

me. I was able to catch a glimpse of Alexandrou in the back, but I didn't see Dimitri. My heart sank. If he was still in that hospital, they would cancel our hearing again.

I finally rode to B'abda in an open jeep. The sun was out, and I felt bathed in its healing rays. Dimitri would be there after all, I told myself. Everything was going to be all right.

I arrived at the courthouse and was put into one of the underground holding cells again. I was still in prison, but I was away from Sanayeh. It was like making a little exit in the right direction. I went upstairs, full of anticipation. Mary was there, and Bob, but no Dimitri.

"Case postponed. January 18."

The clerk made the announcement in Arabic, and Mary translated for me. I squeezed her hand hard and tried to smile. But I felt like finding a little corner where I could roll up in a ball like a sow bug and wait for somebody to step on me.

The next day, all the uncertainties I had tried to bottle up came crashing in on me, and I went to see Mona again. "You've got to help me," I begged. "I'm so nervous. I think I'm losing my mind." I was also afraid I was pregnant, but I didn't tell her that.

She gave me more tranquilizers. It became easier and easier to let the little pills work their magic as I escaped into an apathetic stupor and learned how it felt not to care about a thing. After lockup every night, we smoked hash together, and once again the flickering candlelight would soften the walls, and we would dream of warm, sunny places.

But when morning came, things always seemed worse than ever. I didn't want to see anyone or speak to anyone when I woke up, not even to say good morning. Not until I had had another pill. By Christmas I was tranquilized most of the time and growing more and more dependent on the little pills that mellowed my disposition and allowed me to dream sweet dreams.

During the holiday season whenever Bob and Jessie came to visit, they brought treats. In guilty response, we all tried to stir ourselves out of our general stupor and work on handmade cards.

We wanted Esther to come for Christmas breakfast, and the only way to get privileges in Sanayeh was to do extras for the guards—to bribe them in subtle ways. So I decided to try to make individual taffy cakes. Hanni was in a mellow mood and granted me the extra kitchen time, probably because she thought she would get something out of it.

I would go to the kitchen and prepare the cakes for baking, then sit so the sun's rays came through the window on my face—doing nothing, not even thinking—waiting for the cakes to cook. I wrapped them in foil and tied them with red ribbons. It took a long time for me to do it, for I worked slowly. It was the only way I could work these days.

On Christmas Eve, Mary came, bringing chocolates and good wishes. Bob and Jessie brought a Christmas package for Aiya and her baby, a package for Suzanne, and for me a Francis Schaeffer book they hoped I would enjoy.

When Esther came for breakfast on Christmas

morning, she brought the food for our dinner. That day, we all tried to act happy and forget the stark gray walls around us. But I couldn't. To me, there was nothing cheerful about this day. For it was Christmas, and I was spending it in prison.

CHAPTER

17

The first of the year came and went, and I knew that I was not pregnant. "O God, thank you for that!" I didn't want Dimitri's baby. I looked at Aiya comforting little Andre, and I knew I didn't want any baby. Not now.

There was new leadership in the prison, but conditions didn't improve, and security got tighter than ever. The male *ra'eb* had been replaced by a female *mudeera*—a large, muscular directress who could come into our rooms at any hour of the day or night and demand to know what was going on. She was addicted to searches.

"Basarah! Basarah!" The guards would come running down the hall, telling us to get a move on. They wanted us to hide all our *memnuas* (forbidden objects) because the guards were the ones who would get into trouble if they were found. Up until now, most of the searches had

been halfhearted ones, and all the objects that were taken away, like small mirrors and scissors, could be reclaimed from the office the next morning. But now, the *mudeera's* men would tear up our rooms, going through all our boxes and throwing our clothes on the floor, making a terrible racket and an awful mess and acting as if they enjoyed every minute of it.

Day by day, the tensions grew. One of the women in room one had a baby, and her screams and the ensuing commotion gave us all a sleepless night. The next day, an Arab woman's life was threatened by another inmate, and the *mudeera* said she was going to put the offender in with us.

And then there was Suzanne. Her general slovenliness was becoming more than we could bear. It was impossible to enjoy dinner when she ate with us. And she seldom offered to help with the cooking.

"I'm sick to death of her laziness," I told Anne, and at last she agreed. We put our heads together and came up with a plan to ignore her completely at mealtimes. Anne, Aiya, Penny, and I would prepare our own separate dinners and eat them at our mats.

When Suzanne sauntered in at dinnertime the first night, she looked around in bewilderment. "Where's *my* food?" she demanded.

Anne looked directly at her. "If you want to eat, you can cook your own food and eat by yourself. Or you can start helping us without always being told. We're tired of doing all the cooking for ourselves and for you, too."

Suzanne went into a panic. She raged at us, muttered to herself, and finally sat in a corner and sulked. But she didn't fix a thing for herself to eat. When she realized that we were really going to ignore her, she went to bed.

But the next day she was ready to talk. "Look," she said, "I'll cook dinner for you if you want me to. I'll cook the whole thing."

"When?" Anne was determined to pin her down.

"Well . . . tonight, I guess."

"That's not enough, Suzanne. We've been doing your work around here for a long time."

When the conversation ended, Suzanne had agreed to cook dinner every night for the next two weeks. We thought we had won a victory, but she ran to Esther with a distorted version of the story, making us look like slave drivers. No matter how much we tried to explain, Suzanne always seemed to come out on top. It was just one more pressure that we couldn't control.

On top of everything else, the gas that was used in the kitchen stove went out, and there was no way to replace it because of the war. This meant there was no way to cook—not even to heat water. Outside, the rain fell in torrents of icy water; inside, we felt sure we would freeze to death. The idea of getting through the rest of the winter on cold food and cold bath water put us in a state of near panic.

The trustees had a little bit of kerosene, which they used to heat water for coffee for themselves and for the guards. But there wasn't enough for us. We tried to rig up a heating contraption of our own by stealing olive oil out of the kitchen and pouring it into a little flat tin can. Into that we put a wad of cotton—with the tip soaked with kerosene—and lit it. Then we put slightly larger tin cans on each side to hold a still larger can over the flame. This way we could heat water for coffee.

We had to hide the thing in the bathroom because it was illegal, but we couldn't hide it very well because of the black smoke that came pouring out of it. It took a long time for the water to heat, but it was better than nothing. The problem was that we had to keep stealing oil, and the penalty for stealing was solitary confinement.

I knew that the trustees had a little electric hot plate that they were able to use, and I wondered if we could get permission from the *mudeera* for Esther to bring us one, too.

My heart was pounding when I went to ask her. She had flashy, evil eyes that could switch on and off—liking you one minute and angry the next. This time we were more than lucky. We could have a hot plate, she said, on one condition: We had to agree to stay locked in our room to use it. Supposedly, the only excuse for wanting to be unlocked in this weather was to go to the kitchen. If we had everything we needed in the room, she figured we could just stay there. We agreed.

Esther obliged by bringing the hot plate. But operating it wasn't all that simple. Soon after we began using it the *mudeera* raged into our room, screaming, "Turn that thing off! It caused a blowout. You can use it from now on only in the kitchen!"

We waited, hoping that she would forget all about it. And that night we plugged it into the ceiling outlet in the bathroom. It wasn't easy. I put on my highest heels and stood on tiptoe while one of the girls climbed on my shoulders to reach it. Once we got it plugged in, we left it that way, only unplugging it from the unit.

I would get up at four o'clock each morning and start the water heating for our precious morning coffee, and we kept it going almost all day long to dilute the cold water for our baths.

For a while, my face had begun to clear up a little, but now it was as bad as ever. Any emotional upset seemed to trigger a fresh batch of pimples and boils. Some mornings I would wake up and feel my face throbbing. There was only one thing I could do. Take another tranquilizer and try not to think about it.

One of the foreigners returned from her day in court and was forced by the *mudeera* to undergo a lengthy and humiliating search of all her bodily orifices. I was horrified. Would the *mudeera* do that to me after my next court date a week from now? I felt violated just thinking about it and reached for my tranquilizers. My hands were beginning to tremble whenever I was without a tranquilizer for any length of time. I needed something quick to help me relax, I told myself. It was the only way I could survive in here.

It's not surviving, a voice inside me said. *It's*

hiding. You're getting hooked, Marti. You're getting hooked.

I knew it was true. I couldn't go on like this—just living until it was time for the next pill. I had to pull myself together. I would remain calm. I would practice relaxing. I would find a way to get outside and let the sun fill me with its healing warmth.

But the winter sun was not bright enough to warm me. I moaned softly and hugged myself around the middle, holding a pill clenched tightly in my fist. I was cold, so cold. The pills were the only things that could make me feel safe and warm again. Safe and warm.

And trapped.

The tranquilizers were a trap. A prison worse than Sanayeh. I had to get off of them. But how? I had always thought I could take care of myself. But I was so tired—so very tired. Sometimes I could hardly think. I didn't want to think. It was too painful to let my mind focus in on the person I was letting myself become.

Then work. Get busy with your hands.

I reluctantly put the little pill back on the shelf above my mat, leaving it where I could find it easily if I had to have it. Then I began to "stiggle"—organizing my clothes, moving my boxes and cleaning behind them, putting them back and arranging what was in them.

There, in a corner where I had put it the day Laurel left the prison, was the book she had given me. *Love in the Words and Life of Jesus.* I didn't have any intention of reading it. Preaching was something I didn't need right now. But I opened it curiously and flipped through the pages. I supposed I owed Laurel that much for leaving it with me. It was a fancy gift book with a Scripture verse on one page and a picture or sculpture on the next. It wasn't as threatening as I thought it would be—certainly not heavy reading—and the pictures were lovely. I sat down and began to look at them, turning the pages slowly. It was such a beautiful book, and there was so little beauty around me. The morning passed, and I didn't take the little pill that sat conveniently on the shelf.

Each morning after that, I would awaken as I always did, before the rest of the girls, and pick up the book, just to look at the pictures. Once in a while, I would glance at a verse, and the words seemed to have a beauty, too—a melody that calmed me like a soft song. It was like reading poetry, I thought. I didn't always understand it, but I kept coming back for more.

I began to call it the "*Love Book.*" It was like a gift that had been waiting to be opened until I needed it. It let me feel a gentle beauty, taste a kind of peacefulness that those little pills hadn't offered. I put the tranquilizers away, and I determined never to take them again.

Penny and Anne could hardly talk of anything but my release. There was no doubt in any of our minds that I would be getting out. It wouldn't be long now. In a few days I would go to court again—and I would see Dimitri. I had received one letter and knew that he was miserable. But he still loved me. How I needed to hear those words!

My sweet love, Marti . . . During the rare oc-
casions you are not with me in my thoughts,
I try to read, but it is very difficult, because I
am surrounded by filthy, uneducated, un-
civilized people. They have sharp elbows and
are nauseous to me. The only thing I want
out of life now is to make you happy. We will
be together to the end. For my sake, if not
your own, look after yourself. Don't forget,
you are my everything in life. I send you my
everlasting love. Your man—Dimitri.

I held his letter to my heart, remembering the man I had met in Athens. It seemed so very long ago.

January 18 came. I woke up early and looked at my bad skin in the mirror. It took a long time, but I tried very hard to cover the terrible spots with makeup and camouflage the dark circles under my eyes. I packed a bag of food and some cigarettes for Dimitri and took my yoga book along as a distraction from the foul smell of B'abda.

I hurried toward the truck, anxious to see him, eager to hear his words of love and reassurance. He was there, and he looked better than before. But he was in a terrible mood. There were no words of comfort, no expressions of love, no kisses. Instead, he argued with the guards, cursing loudly at them, agitating them in every way he could.

"Dimitri, stop it! You're only making it harder on yourself." I reached out to touch him on the arm, but he shrugged me away.

"I hate everybody!" he muttered angrily. "I would kill those dirty mongrels if I could! Listen Marti, I'll go on a hunger strike if I have to. I'll get so sick that they'll have to send me back to the hospital. At least there I'll have TV, cigarettes, and a real bed. If they don't send me back, I'll starve to death. I don't care if I do. It's one way to get out of that lousy, stinking Ramal!"

"Oh, Dimitri, don't talk like that. I don't want you to hurt yourself. I care about you, darling. This can't last forever. If you think Ramal is bad, let me tell you about Sanayeh."

But he didn't want to listen. He didn't even want to hear about what I had been through. I was beginning to wonder if this was the same man who had written me that letter of love.

"If it wasn't for that stupid brother of mine," he said, "I would still be in the hospital. He could have made better arrangements for me. He could have gotten more money. But he wouldn't make one simple little deal."

"I don't want to hear anything about deals," I snapped. "Not ever!"

We sat in silence until we reached B'abda, where we were separated again and put into the holding cells. It was eleven o'clock before we were taken upstairs, and we had to wait in the courtroom until three-thirty for our turn.

Dimitri sat next to me, and we were able to talk a little on the sly. "You shouldn't have given them my name at customs," he said. "If I had stayed on the outside, you would be out by now." He was nervously tapping his heels against the floor—up, down, up, down—over and over. "You shouldn't have hired that woman lawyer. You should have given me the money instead. We would both be out by now."

I hardly knew what to say. He was blaming the whole thing on me! Was this the man I had fallen in love with—the man who was going to take care of me and make my life complete?

Suddenly his mood changed. "Marti," he whispered, "we'll forget all this when we get out. We'll go away together. Just you and me alone. I hate people, Marti. Really hate them. But not you—I want to be with you and nobody else."

I felt uncomfortable, unsure of my feelings. Could I live a life like that? Alone with Dimitri, while he hated the rest of the world? It was a relief when the proceedings started.

Mary's defense was lengthy, and she had more information involving Alexandrou and Leonidas. But nothing was decided. We would have to wait until January 31 for the verdict.

Dimitri reassured me. "We'll get out. I can tell. The lawyers have already arranged it." Mary was hopeful, too. January 31, I thought. That was less than two weeks away. Only two more weeks of my life to be spent in Sanayeh.

CHAPTER

18

When I returned to Sanayeh, I was told that Suzanne had been taken to the hospital. "She was hemorrhaging," Anne told me, "and was probably having a miscarriage." I should have been sorry, but I knew Suzanne hadn't wanted the baby, and I couldn't help rejoicing in her absence. It was so much more peaceful in the room without her.

"Do you want to sign this card that Penny and I are sending her?" asked Anne. I shook my head. There wasn't any use pretending that I cared—when I didn't.

Aiya and Andre were released early one morning, leaving only the three of us in the room together. Penny and Anne went to court again, and we were all excited and full of great plans as we waited for our verdicts. Oh, we would get out. There was no doubt about it. Perhaps we would all go to Switzerland, to a retreat we had heard about called L'Abri. Then we would visit London together—maybe Rome, before we parted for our homes. We talked constantly about how great it was going to be. When we were tired of talking, we moved our mats and belongings to one side of the room—the best side— so that no matter how many people came into the room, we would be where we wanted to be.

In the newfound peacefulness of the room, I began to draw again—for the first time in quite a while I felt that I was able. The winter sun seemed suddenly warmer, and sometimes I sat in the courtyard, resting and feeling good. Nothing would get me down now, I told myself. I had hit the bottom and bounced back. The road was smooth, and the future looked good.

But not for long.

The room began to fill again. That wasn't so bad—it was something you grew to expect. We pushed things aside and made a little more room. But one afternoon, several days before I was to go back to court, we heard Hanni's doglike voice growling out in the hall. She stopped at our room and kicked the door open, slamming it back against the wall. She was obviously angry, with a look of disgust on her face, and it was frightening to see her that way. She stood with her hands on her hips, surveying the room for a full minute. None of us moved. Only when she stepped aside and took her huge bulk out of the doorway, could we see who was standing behind her.

Madame Chevalier was back! And with another new girl named Sonyia. Hanni pushed and kicked and banged until all their things were in the room, then slammed out, crashing the door against the wall again.

"I want to be in the corner," Chevy announced. "I don't want this space in the middle of the room. One of you will have to trade with me."

We looked at each other and shook our heads. I was frantic at the thought of having her in the room again, and I sure wasn't going to let her start bossing us around. I sat down on my mat and waited, and Anne and Penny did the same.

At last Chevy arranged her things in the center of the floor. I watched her, hating the smug way she looked at us, despising the sound of her voice. She was already starting that old song again: "My poor back. You don't know how I suffer. I might as well be dead. Just consider me dead."

She said it over and over—again and again. My mind tightened. I could feel my muscles tense. I couldn't stand her being here—I couldn't stand her at all. Suddenly I leaped to my feet.

All right! I *would* consider her dead. I would bury her, so none of us would have to see her at all. I snatched some extra sheets from the corner. There were already ropes strung across the room. I strung another and began throwing the sheets over them, surrounding Chevy—boxing her in. Then I grabbed a big needle, threaded it, and started sewing up the seams, attaching the sheets tightly to the ropes so that she would be encased. She would be an island unto herself, and she would be blocked from our view.

Chevy didn't say a single word while I was

working. She just sat on her mat and chewed on her bottom lip. Anne and Penny watched me in amazement. But they didn't say anything either. "There!" I stood back and surveyed my job with satisfaction. "Now we can do just what you have been asking us to do, Madame Chevalier. We can consider you dead!"

She sat there chewing on her lip until she had to go to the bathroom. Then she stood up and ripped a portion of sheeting away. She looked at me and swore—loud, vulgar words that would have shocked and frightened me a few months before. "You can't do that to me!" she shouted. "This is not some kind of private hotel. This is prison, and I have my rights!"

But the rest of the sheeting stayed up, even though it made our room look like some kind of hippy camp. Sonyia, the new girl, was bewildered, and Anne and Penny looked a little confused, too. I was exhausted, and didn't even care when the Arab kitchen girls passed our room one by one and sneered, "Foreigners no good!"

The next morning, we began to realize that something else was wrong at the prison. *Sit* Marie and *Sit* Samya came to the room, hinting mysteriously at trouble ahead. "Maybe take away all privileges. Maybe unlock door—maybe not." They spoke to Chevy in Arabic, but evidently didn't tell her any more than they told us. Something had obviously happened. But what? What could anyone have done that was bad enough to keep us all locked up?

The noise began at the end of the hall. A great clatter of voices and thumping of feet and doors crashing open. *Crash! Bang! Smash!* The *mudeera*, Hanni, and some of the other guards stormed into our room for a surprise search. They sent us out into the hall while they threw our clothes and food in every direction. They searched through everything, not missing a crack or a corner, and they took big sacks full of *memnua* items.

"Why? Why?" we asked, and they finally told us. Two girls who were being released last night had been caught trying to smuggle hashish out in their mouths—and now we were all under suspicion.

I watched them leave with what I hoped was a look of scorn. I was going to court in three days, and then they could all go to blazes. I reorganized my things for what I was sure was the last time, then packed most of them away in my suitcase, ready to leave. I was really angry about only one thing—they had taken the medicine I had been using on my face.

January 31 came at last, and the truck arrived to take me to B'abda for the verdict. Despite the way Dimitri had spoken to me the last time we were in court together, I looked forward to seeing him again—to riding close beside him in the truck. Today would be a new day in our lives. I would never forget any of this, I told myself. But at last, it was almost over. We could forget the past and make plans for the future.

But Dimitri looked terrible—pale, thin, unshaven, wrinkled, worried. And he sounded even worse. "Why hasn't my lawyer been to see me?" he wanted to know. "And why does my brother keep coming when he never does a thing I tell him?''

He stopped complaining only long enough to take the food and cigarettes I had brought for him, then he went right on. ''Why did you spend a thousand dollars if you're not sure you're getting out? I told you that you should have given the money to me. Listen, Marti, I want you to promise me—if you get out and I don't, be sure and send me money. And do something about that face of yours, why don't you!''

That did it! ''Don't you dare talk to me about my face, Dimitri Strongilis. It looks like this because I'm in prison, and that's because of you.''

''Don't blame your problems on me, Marti.'' His voice was bitter, hard. ''If you had kept your sweet mouth shut about my name, they would never have picked me up, and I would have had you out of here by now.''

''I don't see how you could have helped me when you were trying to run away.''

He ignored that and sat in silence a few seconds. When he spoke again, I couldn't believe what I was hearing. ''If this case has to go to the appeals court, I want you to change lawyers. I want us to have the same one. If you refuse, I'll testify against you.''

I was stunned. And this, I thought, was the same man who was asking me to send him money when I got out of prison. He was asking me to wait for him so we could spend our lives together.

''Never mind,'' he said, shaking his head. ''It's

finished. It's all over." He was right, I thought. It really was.

We arrived at B'abda and were met by a surprised guard. "No court today. Everything closed. Is Moslem holiday."

I heard a moan and realized it had come from me. Why hadn't somebody told us? Why had they let us wait and hope and come here, only to be told to go back to prison and wait? Dimitri and I rode back in the same truck, but we were as silent as two strangers. There was really nothing more for either of us to say. Dimitri, I thought, had said it all.

Early the next morning, the Paeths came to see me. I ran eagerly up front, sure that they must have news. They probably had heard my verdict and wanted to be the first to tell me. I greeted them with smiles. My suitcase was packed. I was ready to go.

"Have you heard?" I asked them.

"Haven't you been told?" Bob answered back. His face looked shocked. There was concern in his eyes.

I swallowed hard. "Have—have I been sentenced?"

Bob nodded. "I'm sorry, Marti."

Back in the States, my mother was reading a brief telegram. "February 1, 1975. Martha convicted. Three years."

I felt faint and bit my lips hard, determined to keep control of myself. Slowly, I turned and walked back to my room. There was a buzzing in my ears as I sat down cross-legged in my corner and leaned my head against the wall. I didn't want to talk to anyone, but word soon spread throughout the prison. There were no secrets in those walls.

Alia appeared and put her arms around me. Her voice was soft and gentle as she spoke in Arabic, trying to comfort me. I recognized one word: *"afu"* ("amnesty"). She said it again and again.

But amnesty was almost eleven months away. I began to cry and shake my head. And then I remembered that Alia was facing life in prison for a crime she hadn't committed, with no chance of release. What a selfish pig I was. I put my head on her shoulder and sobbed. My tears were for both of us.

In spite of my personal trauma, the prison routine continued, building tension upon tension until our nerves were as fragile as a pack of cards, stacked high and ready to fall.

A new commandant came to our room for another inspection, took one look at the rag that we kept in front of the door to wipe our feet on and snapped, "Filthy! Disease!"

Then he turned and left, his head held high and his nose wrinkled in distaste. I was humiliated, for I prided myself on the cleanliness of our room. I took the rag and soaked it, pounding and scrubbing, trying to get it clean. It was useless. The stains remained. It was, I thought, just one more thing I couldn't seem to control.

Anne and Penny brought me news that made me feel even worse. Suzanne was returning. The thought of her in the same room with me was almost more than I could stand. It had been bad enough to have her there when I thought I would be leaving. Now it was intolerable. I forgot all about the contract I had made.

"If I'm going to serve out my time," I told the others, "I can't survive with this constant friction between Suzanne and me. One of us has to go."

We couldn't bar her from the room, we decided, but we could bar her from our lives. We decided to ostracize her completely, not even acknowledging that she was there. It was better that way for all of us.

When she came back, we told her. "It's just too much tension, Suzanne, when we try to eat with you. We've all tried it before, and you know it doesn't work."

"You can't be nice to me, can you, Marti? Not even when I've lost my baby." Her lip was quivering, and I looked away. She wasn't going to change my mind with any of her clever little tricks. She sat on her mat and watched us as we hung still another sheet separating our side of the room from hers. Evidently tired, she lay down and turned her face to the wall.

Doris Dodge, an American who had made contact with us through the embassy and had visited us often, came to see Suzanne. After a few minutes, I was called up front. When I walked into the visiting room, she was waiting.

"Marti, how could you do this?" she demanded. "Suzanne is a human being. What on earth is the matter with you?"

I shrugged. I was a little shaken by her criticism, but she just didn't understand. She couldn't.

"We all feel that it's better this way. It's the only way there can be any peace in the room."

Doris shook her head angrily. "It's murderous the way you are treating her. You are killing her from the inside out. That girl came out of the hospital full of resolutions to do more work and try harder to get along, and you won't even give her a chance!"

The criticism didn't stop with Doris. Word leaked out about my treatment of Suzanne. On the next visiting day, the questions flew.

"Marti, how would you feel if you were in Suzanne's place?" Bob asked me. "Eating alone, blocked off by sheets, with nobody who wants to talk to you?"

"You just don't understand . . ." I kept trying to tell people, but nobody would listen.

"Marti, are you feeling all right? Is something bothering you that you want to talk about?" Esther came to see me. Her face showed her concern.

And then I heard the ugly rumors, brought back from the visitors by Suzanne herself and whispered to Anne and Penny, who promptly told me. "Marti isn't handling herself well, is she? It's probably because of her conviction. Poor thing. She is showing all the symptoms of paranoia . . . mentally disturbed . . . needs help. . . ."

Anne and Penny wrote long letters to Esther trying to explain the tension Suzanne had been causing for months, while I just sat and fumed. Whom did they think they were talking about? Mentally disturbed, indeed! I was the director of a mental health clinic. I was the most rational, sane person in this whole miserable place. Nobody appreciated how hard I worked—how hard I tried. And Suzanne was getting the best of me after all. If I wasn't nice to her, she would run and tell Doris, Esther, and the Paeths, and they would stop caring for me. It was blackmail. Dirty blackmail. How I hated her for it!

In the midst of this turmoil, Irene arrived. She was an Iranian woman who called herself a princess. She was short and grossly fat and wrapped herself in her mink coat the way other women used bathrobes. She strode into our room one day and demanded, "Give me a space!"

A newcomer demanding a space. Especially one this size! What a laugh. Something inside me snapped. I would show this woman. People around here would have to realize that I wasn't going to run around waiting on them anymore. From now on, I was going to worry about myself. *My* comfort and peace in this prison—*my* feelings—*my* face—would come first.

"You must be in the wrong room," I told her. "There isn't any room for you here." She looked at me in surprise. Maybe she didn't speak English. I waved my hands at her and pointed to the door. "Go on . . . go on. Get out!"

But this woman wasn't like Suzanne. She didn't lie down and turn her face to the wall. "You mean, ugly American!" she spat. And she reached out and started pulling the clothes and sheets down from the ropes, throwing them onto the floor and walking on them.

I was furious. But when I looked at Anne and

Penny for support, I saw the puzzled looks on their faces. "You know, Marti," Anne said softly, "I do believe if Penny and I came into the prison now, you wouldn't even be helpful to us."

"Oh, no," I protested. "No . . . that's not true. You two are my friends."

But it was true. In the beginning I had bustled around to find blankets and sheets for new girls, making sure they had food, introducing them. . . .

What had happened to me? I was mean and selfish and rude. Everything I did was the reflection of a cold, hardhearted woman. Instinctively, I began to blame all my problems on Suzanne and the prison. But were they really her fault? I went to bed early that night and lay with my eyes closed, pretending to sleep. But I was wide awake long after the last candle had gone out. Awake and afraid. Something was happening to me. Something terrible. There were moments when I didn't care if I lived or not—and those moments were coming more and more often. I felt as if I were in the bottom of a deep pit, hanging onto the end of a frayed rope . . . the end of my rope.

Oh, help, somebody. Somebody pull me up before I drown!

CHAPTER

19

In the morning, I awakened early, as usual. Up until now, I had gone immediately to the door, putting my face into the little hatch and looking to see who was on duty in the hallway. Then I would begin the agonizing daily routine of trying to get the door unlocked. The responsibility was always mine because I was the first one up.

If I knew the guard, I would call her by name. "Hanni, please unlock the door! *Min fadlik, iftahi al-bab!*"

Some mornings I would call until my throat felt dry and rough, and my voice was hoarse. The guards could hear me, but they only listened when they felt like it. If one of them was in the mood to let me out, she would. Or she might say, *"Ba'ad shwey"* ("Later—I'll take care of you later"). Sometimes she ignored me for several hours, while I stood there and begged until I was close to tears.

This morning, I was just too tired and depressed to care. I felt a weight around me, like a load I was carrying on my back. And I resented feeling this way. I had tried hard to keep my spirits up. I had worked hard, too—harder than any of the other girls. But I didn't get any satisfaction from the work I did. Only a crazy compulsion to do more. And I expected everybody else to do more, too.

I glanced around the room, letting my gaze fall on each sleeping body. Look at them—all of them—sleeping their lives away. They expected to lie in their beds and rest every morning while good old Marti yelled at the guards until someone unlocked the door. Well, I was glad I wasn't like them!

Tears came to my eyes. They had made me feel so guilty last night. They didn't know how tired I was—tired of responsibility, tired of living with people I hated, tired of living at all in this prison. I wiped away the tears and clenched my fists. "O God," I muttered. "O God, what have I done to be brought so low?"

There was no answer. There never seemed to be an answer when I talked to God. Nothing concrete I could put my arms around and hold onto.

I reached for the little book that Laurel had left me. The *Love Book*. It always calmed me to look at the pictures—to hear in my mind the rhythm of the words. I turned the pages idly, found one I liked, and stopped.

Jesus told about two men. One was a Pharisee—a successful, respected man, and the other was a publican—a tax collector, disliked by everyone. The Pharisee was proud, distinguished, a man who knew his own identity.

I could really relate to that, I thought. Especially when he said in prayer, "God, I thank thee that I am not like other men. . . ."

I knew exactly how he felt. I was glad I wasn't like Suzanne, or Chevy, or any of the other prison women, except my few special friends. I was better than that. And I was thankful for it.

> *But the tax collector, standing far off, would not even lift up his eyes . . . saying, "God, be merciful to me a sinner!"*

That was Suzanne. A miserable sinner! She ought to ask for mercy. But I didn't think she'd get any, for she didn't deserve it. I was glad I'd opened up this little book this morning. It was just the tonic I needed after last night's humbling experience. I continued reading.

> *I tell you, this man went down to his house justified rather than the other; for every one who exalts himself will be humbled, but he who humbles himself will be exalted* (Luke 18:11–14, RSV).

I sat there in silence, staring at the words on the page. I read them again, thinking I had made a mistake. Suzanne was justified, and I was not? I closed the book. I closed my eyes. A wave of nausea swept over me. The Pharisee was not the winner after all, and neither was I.

I thought of the way I had treated Suzanne and Chevy, my coldness to people I didn't like, my lies and protestations of innocence to everyone I knew. The faces of people I'd hurt paraded before me: my mother and father; the people at the counseling center; friends I'd lied to; the people who had faithfully visited me in Sanayeh, listening to my troubles, believing in me. I recalled the day Doris Dodge had been so angry with me. I knew that she was right. I had wanted Suzanne out of our room so badly that I was murderous. I could have killed her. I thought of the other women in prison who had already committed murder. I was no better than the rest.

What was the matter with me? What sort of a person had I become?

I was glad nobody else in the room was awake. I didn't want to talk to anyone. I didn't want to have to look them in the face. I just sat there and wanted to die.

No one stirred. The door was locked, and we were all crowded into this little room together. But I was alone. Totally alone. I put my head into my hands. Oh, if it all could only go away and be forgotten and wash into the sand and sea and be no more.

And be no more . . . and be no more. . . .

How I wished it could be no more. I didn't see how I could live with these feelings of guilt any longer.

Then get rid of them.

But how? I asked myself. How could I take what had already happened out of my life? What was done was done. The past couldn't be changed.

But the future can.

How could I face the future when my mind was full of yesterday? How could I ever be free?

Forgive. . . .

Forgiveness. My mind raced back—back to the time when I was a child. Such easy faith I had had in those years! My parents loved me. God loved me. I never doubted it. Forgiveness was as easy as saying I was sorry and meaning it. And then I was forgiven. And I wasn't punished for it anymore.

Bible verses about Jesus came to my mind. Especially John 3:16: "For God so loved the world. . . ." I closed my eyes and remembered. It had been a promise. God loved me enough to forgive me. He would forgive—my guilt would be washed away—and it would be no more.

And be no more . . . and be no more.

Tears came to my eyes, slipped over the lids, ran down my cheeks. I sat there, feeling weak, my strength depleted, my will no longer my own. There were so many things to feel remorse for. They loomed before me like a giant kaleidoscope, twisting and turning, painting the many colors of my life. It would take years, I thought— years and years of making amends. Where on earth would I start?

With yourself, Marti. Ask me to forgive you.

I sat on my mat in the light of early morning and wondered if I could—as unworthy and undeserving as I was. It was sunrise over Sanayeh, but it was still midnight in my heart, for I didn't like the person I had become. I struggled with the thought for a long, long time. I had become hateful, despicable. How could I ever hope to be forgiven? How could I ever hope to change?

It won't be easy.

I nodded. That was the truth. It was so hard to change. I anguished over the things that I had done—but I wasn't sure that I wouldn't do them again. I hated the terrible feelings I had toward Suzanne—but I still didn't like her. It would be lying to say that I did. I was deeply grieved that I had lost my temper and put sheets around Chevy, but I felt justified when she was hidden from my view. It made me miserable to know that I had lied to the people who cared about me—but I still wanted them to believe that I was innocent.

I felt a pain inside. A sick, deep pain. As though I were gasping for breath but couldn't breathe. I wondered if this was the way people felt when they were having mental breakdowns. I was out of control, out of orbit, spinning wildly on some uncharted course, through universes unknown to man.

"Save me, Jesus!" I whispered, and then I began to sob, my shoulders shaking with uncontrollable weeping. "Lord God—heavenly Father—forgive me of all my wrongdoings. I am so undeserving. I don't merit your forgiveness. But I have no strength of my own, and if you do not save me now, I will surely die."

Oh, if God would only give me some sign. If he could only show me that he heard me—that he was listening to my prayer!

The room was silent. Slowly, very slowly, the sleeping bodies began to waken, moaning softly, turning over on their mats. The daily routine of Sanayeh was beginning. But today the early morning light brightened, intensified, illuminating the room with a glow—with a warmth—that I had never felt before. I sat quietly and waited, the *Love Book* closed upon my lap. An unexpected gentleness filled me, and I looked around the room at the other girls, seeing each one of them as if for the first time. Everything was vivid, as if someone had dusted away the gray fog that had filled my mind. Colors were bright. Outlines were distinct. I closed my eyes and opened them again. I felt as if an electrical current had passed through me, suddenly turning me on. Yet I was quiet—and peaceful. The terrible guilt that had boiled inside me like a fever was gone. Something was happening, and I knew that it was good.

Anne crawled out from under her covers and staggered to her feet. She stretched and yawned, then she went to the door and tried to open it. She would have to call the guards this morning, I thought. Because I couldn't. I could do nothing but sit there on the floor and hug my newfound peacefulness close to my heart.

But Anne didn't call the guards. She pushed the door open and walked out. It was unlocked. Someone had walked by and turned the key without any help from me.

I closed my eyes and felt the tears escape. I had thought I was alone, but he had been there all the time. "Oh, Father," I whispered, "thank you." For I knew that God was not silent . . . not even in Sanayeh.

CHAPTER

20

I began sketching again. At first it was idle doodling, something to keep me from being so preoccupied with my mindless, compulsive cleaning. But one day Rahaili returned to the prison, and I felt as if I had been given a second chance. I knew that her ten years would soon be up, and she would be leaving for good, so I began drawing her—working hard to capture that elusive dignity that I saw in her face.

Soon my work began to give me a sense of accomplishment. It helped me begin to feel good about myself again, and before long I was sketching the prison, capturing all of its details. For some reason, recording it on a piece of paper made it a little easier to bear.

Every morning I spent some devotional time reading the *Love Book*. I read and reread, thinking about the passages and trying to sort them out . . . feeling my way through a galaxy of emotions I didn't yet comprehend. Those early morning hours gave me peace for the day—a chance to pray quietly to my heavenly Father, whose presence I felt right beside me.

Before, when people had given me books, I had only looked through them because I felt obliged. But now I couldn't seem to read enough. Once I started, I couldn't stop. I had never been an avid reader before, but now it was as if a previously unrealized hunger was daily being filled. I read with an appetite and kept a notebook and pen beside me, making voluminous notes and writing down questions to think about later.

I started exercising, too, toning up flabby muscles, taking off accumulated inches that only made me feel sluggish and fat. My face seemed to be slightly better. Some of the boils had subsided. I tried to keep my fingers from scratching and waited anxiously for the sun.

The warmer days finally came, bringing hot, dry winds from the Libyan desert, and sunshine in the courtyard. I went there as often as I could, wanting to be alone, yearning for enough quiet time to think things out. I knew how wrong I had been. My spirit told me that. But I made no attempt to go to the people I had wronged and try to make things right. I didn't know if it would make a difference, and I didn't know how to start.

Daily, for hours, I sat on my mat and assumed the yoga lotus position, with my hands out, palms upward. Everyone thought I was meditating, but I was praying—cataloguing my faults

234

and problems, listing them one by one, holding them mentally in my outstretched hands. "Father, this is the way I am. Forgive me, and help me be really different," I would say.

I knew I was forgiven. But could I ever be free of the wrong patterns I had established—from the hate that I felt toward Suzanne and others who hurt me?

The answer came. Learning to love others as I loved myself wasn't going to be a gift. It would be an arduous battle, but I would have the victory. And I knew it wouldn't take place deep inside of me while I meditated and read—I was to be put right back on the firing line, dealing with people.

The quiet serenity of my early morning reading was shattered one morning when the door crashed open, and a new girl was thrown into our room. She staggered and fell to her knees, then collapsed and lay motionless on her side. Her eyes were open, staring hideously, and her breaths came in agonizing gulps. Suddenly, she was quiet.

The other girls were sitting up on their mats, still half asleep, stunned by the intrusion. I was the only one awake enough to move quickly. In a panic, I ran for Alia. "Come quick!" I shouted. "Do something! Hurry up!"

Before we got back to the room, we knew the girl was still alive, for we could hear her screaming. She had ripped off her sweater and was wrapping it around her neck. The screams turned to painful gurgles as she twisted the sweater tight, cutting off her own breath.

I left Alia and the others to struggle with her the best they could and ran for the *mudeera*. She brought the doctor with her, and between them they screamed at the girl in French, shook her roughly, and forced a pill down her throat.

"What's wrong with her?" I asked. "Is she going to be all right?" Before, I would have wanted no part in her games or in her pain. But now I could look at her as another human being. I could feel compassion for someone else who suffered.

The doctor looked at me and shrugged. "Not to worry," he said. "She is just a little crazy. We will put her in the hospital tomorrow."

Tomorrow! They were leaving us with a suicidal woman who was crazy, and all they could say was, "Tomorrow"? Too stupified to comment, I watched the doctor and the *mudeera* disappear down the corridor. "Not to worry," I repeated, wondering if it was safe to sleep in the room that night.

When I turned, I was astonished to see the new girl standing quietly in the middle of the room. I noticed for the first time her tight jeans, fashionable boots, and tightly cropped hair. She lit a cigarette, inhaling deeply, and gave me a quick smile.

"Pretty good, huh? They always fall for that crazy act. Tomorrow I'll get to go to the hospital—soft beds and TV—and then they'll have to deport me home to France." She sat on the floor and began to work at the heel of her boot.

"My name's Bridget. I've been in and out of

Beirut at least 150 times in the last ten years, always trafficking hash. This time I got too cute, and they caught me. It was humiliating. I felt like a dumb amateur."

She was so cocky, so sure of herself, and such a fake. My heart broke for her, and I prayed quietly, "Oh, Father, please show her your love, and help her find a new way of life."

Then the heel came loose in her hand. It was packed full of hashish—high grade stuff, she told us. The others were ecstatic, but I didn't want anything to do with it. It was a part of my old life, the part I was forgiven for and wanted to forget.

Bridget stayed all night and left early the next morning for the hospital, just as she had planned. Standing at the door with Hanni were two more new girls. For a moment, my heart sank. We had just gotten rid of one, and here came two more. Well, I told myself, we would just have to re-shuffle and rearrange. Before, it had taken so much out of me to be constantly settling people in. The continuous upheaval had been more than I could stand, and I had acted mean and selfish. But now, I seemed to have a new source of strength.

They stood there inside the doorway looking scared and bewildered as I stared at them. One of them tried to smile, but her lips were trembling. "I'm Percy, and this is Mia," she said.

Something in Percy's face reminded me of myself on my first day here—a false assurance that covered panic, a smile that held back tears. It was with a newfound joy that I said, "OK. Come on. Let me show you where you can put your things."

Yet it was still hard to be that civil to Suzanne. She complained and whined as much as ever and made herself thoroughly unlikable. When Laurel and the Paeths both sent food boxes for me to divide, Suzanne stood at my shoulder and whimpered. "You never give me my share. You're always mean to me. . . ."

Each word that came out of her mouth was like rubbing salt into an open wound. I kept quiet and gave her more, but I didn't feel charitable about it. I felt as if I were being blackmailed. If I didn't do as she wanted, she would run and tell, and then everybody would be mad at me all over again.

"Forgive me," I whispered in the darkness that night. "Oh, Father, I'm sorry that I don't love Suzanne. She won't let me like her." Suddenly I couldn't say any more. Was that true? Was I really sorry? Or did I need Suzanne as a kind of scapegoat for all my bad feelings? Were we all using her as a collection pot for our hatred of this place?

Suzanne is someone Jesus died for just like you.

I closed my eyes tighter. I couldn't deny that. I felt convicted. Yet its ramifications stunned me. For it meant that she had as much right to talk to God as I did. And it meant that he cared about her just as much as he cared about me. Was she lying over there right now talking to him with her eyes closed?

I sat up on my mat. The moon was shining, and its light came through the little window, bathing us all in dull silver. I could see Suzanne clearly, lying still, her eyes closed. She looked like a rejected, lost child. And she looked tired, as if her day had been a long one. I felt a lump rise up in my throat and tried to swallow it down.

She seemed so different to me now than she did in the daytime. She seemed pitiful and . . . and mistreated. If I could just remember Suzanne the way she looked now, would it help me ignore her pettiness during the day? If I could think of her like this, as a needy person, maybe I could stop picking at her, pointing out her faults, making her the scapegoat.

I lay down again and closed my eyes. But I didn't go to sleep for a long time, for I kept remembering Suzanne's face, full of pain and rejection. It was a disturbing memory. My mother said that the more unlovable a person was, the more love that person needed. If that were true, then Suzanne needed love and understanding. I thought about it for a long time before I finally fell asleep.

It was time for Anne and Penny to go back to B'abda and receive their verdicts. I watched them leave, knowing just how they felt—nervous and excited, wanting to know the decision—yet not wanting to know either, just in case it was bad. I thought about them all day, waiting for their return. When they finally came in, they were smiling and laughing. "This is it," I thought. "They're going to leave." I wanted to be glad for them. But, oh, how I dreaded being left alone, for the Paeths were leaving me, too, going home to the States in June.

"What happened?" I asked. "You look like you've got good news."

Anne laughed lightly and lit a cigarette. "Our good news was just like yours . . . three years."

I was speechless. How could they take it so lightly? Three years—and neither one of them was shedding a tear. "What's to be gained by crying?" Anne wanted to know. "Poor Nicole is an Arab and isn't eligible for an eighteen-month amnesty like we are. He has to serve his whole time. We've already been here nine months. We're halfway through."

So was I. A little more than halfway, for I had come into Sanayeh a couple of weeks before Anne and Penny had. We would be here together—all the way. I wasn't going to be left alone. I put down a sheet on the floor, made some coffee, and sliced some "uncle's bread." When we added a little jam on top, it almost seemed as though we were celebrating.

But I noticed that they spent the next few days trying to escape the prison in a haze of hashish—generously supplied by the departed Bridget. They offered it to me, and I found it easy to refuse. I had found something better. I didn't need that kind of high anymore.

There was no peace in Beirut that spring—inside the prison or out. When the Paeths came to visit, they brought word of the growing unrest. There was even a chance, Bob said, of civil war. "If widespread fighting breaks out," he told me, "there's a possibility that all foreigners might be granted amnesty and be released." It was a hopeful thought that almost made me feel like praying for war.

But I didn't. I prayed for peace instead. Peace in Beirut, in the prison, in our room, and in me.

So many things—so many people—were now part of my past. Even Dimitri. Yet there was still one person I longed to hear from. The one I always dreamed about. The one who had always been there when I needed him. The wonderful, elusive G. I wanted to hear from him badly because I still thought that I couldn't be without a man in my life.

One afternoon as I was leaving the visitors' room, Mona called my name and handed me a letter. I glanced at the return address. G had finally written. I held the letter against me like a precious treasure. My sister had written that G was asking about me. He would write, she said, when he felt that I was ready to hear from him.

I was ready! Oh, so ready! I opened the envelope carefully. What would he say? What words of love would he finally commit to me? I began to read. Slowly at first, then faster. I reread G's letter three times. Then I folded it carefully and put it back into the envelope. After a year in prison, he had only written a fifteen-line note full of obscure, mystical Oriental phrases.

The war raged on outside, and a small private war raged in my heart. All my old relationships were broken. I was going to have to put my dreams of G aside. I wasn't up to playing games of love with him or anyone else. And I was, for the first time in my life, without a man. Could Jesus really satisfy the longings of my heart and fill all my needs and help me be alone without physical love and affection?

"Oh, Lord, help me to love you and need you more than the men in my life. Come and change my desires and give me new ones. Take this loneliness and pain away."

CHAPTER

21

The civil war was now a fact. By April, it had spread from the mountains to downtown Beirut. It became almost the only thing we talked about, especially on visiting days.

We didn't know it then, but we were caught in the middle of a battle that would rage for many years, killing thousands and destroying the beautiful city. No one would win this conflict. Everyone was a loser, and Beirut was the worst. It was the center—the core. All the anger and strife of Lebanon was capsulized here, tearing the city apart. And we were in the midst of it all.

"There are rumors of evacuating Beirut, just like they had to do in 1858," Esther told us. "I'm not sure if this means that they will release you early or send you to prisons in outlying districts."

We sat in our room that night and lit the candles and listened to the sound of distant gunfire. It was like the thunderstorms of last winter echoing against the darkness, raging until their fury was spent, and then dying away.

But the war didn't die away. "It's getting worse and worse," Esther told us in May. "Now there's a shortage of food in the stores, and people aren't allowed to leave their homes because it's too dangerous. Some have gone to the mountains and barricaded themselves up there. Yesterday I had my sheets hanging on the roof to dry, and when I went to take them down, they were riddled with bullet holes."

Like the rest of Beirut, we were frequently out of fresh fruit, vegetables, and water. Several times, at great inconvenience and danger to themselves, the Paeths would send fresh oranges and lemons for me. These were things I craved, like others craved cigarettes.

I had been without fruit of any kind for over a week when a bag arrived from them. I peeled an orange and sat down to enjoy it, slowly sucking the juice, savoring each drop of sweetness.

Suddenly there was a terrible clattering outside, harsh, loud reports that could only come from automatic weapons. It was machine gun crossfire right outside our window—so close that I expected to see the bullets coming through the walls.

We all panicked, not knowing what to do, which way to go for safety. There were ten of us in the little room by then, and we bumped and staggered, trying to get down into corners, covering our heads with our arms and hunching low.

Mia had evidently experienced this before, for she was the only one who kept her head. "Relax!" she ordered. "Just stay down where you are. It'll be over in a few minutes."

"Close that window!" I yelled.

"Leave it alone!" Mia yelled back. "The glass will just shatter, and we'll all get cut. Get back down against the wall and wait."

The gunfire increased . . . seemed to come closer. It felt like shock waves were passing through my body. "Oh, Father! I don't want to die here. Not in prison, Lord!"

In desperation, we began belly-crawling into the bathroom where we huddled together on the floor until the firing diminished and finally stopped. Then, exhausted from fear and tension, we straggled into our room and collapsed limply on our mats.

Ba—rrrooom!

I grabbed my pillow and held it over my head. My legs were trembling so hard they shook my whole body. I heard Suzanne begin to whimper. Chevy cursed loudly. And somebody in the far corner began to sob. A bomb had exploded in the street just outside our window, and the thick stone walls of Sanayeh trembled like paper in the wind. We were so scared we didn't move, not even to run for a corner. We lay trembling on our mats and heard the windows around the prison explode and shatter from the impact. We

245

listened to the sound of falling glass and the dull thuds of walls crumbling down.

"If we don't get out of this place," Anne said, "we'll all be killed. Let's send messages to our embassies—see if they can try to get us away from here."

"And write letters," Penny added. "If we write everyone we know and ask them to demand our release, it might put enough pressure on the government to get something done."

We sent a note to Esther telling her of our plans, and she came almost immediately. It was the first time I had seen her so visibly shaken by what was going on outside. She had been stopped by young PLO boys with machine guns, and they had pointed the weapons at her until she convinced them she was on legitimate business. We had no idea we were putting her in such danger by asking her to see us.

"I've called your embassies," she said. "They're very concerned about your safety, but they're afraid that if you start making a big fuss, you might all get transferred to one of the prisons outside the city. Listen to me, girls. Those places are awful—much, much worse than Sanayeh. Here, at least you have floors. Out there, it is nothing but dirt, and it's really no safer."

Reluctantly, we tore up the letters we had written. But we couldn't forget the war. It was impossible with the sound of gunfire and exploding shells around us. The army was patrolling right outside our window, and snipers were on our rooftop. Our nerves were all strained to the point of exploding, and we snapped at each other incessantly.

"What's the matter with you?" I shouted at Christian, one of the new girls who had joined us. "That's my wash bucket you just used to clean your dirty clothes in. It's filthy. Look at it. No! No! Don't wipe it out with that sponge. We use that for the dishes. Don't you know how to do anything right?"

Afterward, I was so ashamed. Under pressure, I was letting my old patterns return. I thought about a book I had finished reading—*The Hiding Place* by Corrie ten Boom. If Corrie could be selfless in prison, why couldn't I? I bowed my head and whispered a prayer. "Let it be possible for me, too, Father. Let me be patient and kind, even in these hard times."

It wasn't long before Chevy began her dying routine again. "You don't know how sick I am. Nobody knows. Ohhh. . . ." Then she would hold her back with one hand and moan. Long, dramatic sounds that none of us could imitate. "I haven't long to live. Don't concern yourselves. Just consider me dead."

Penny was too cramped in her corner. The candles were too close to Chevy. Mia was moving all her things and making a mess. When Anne and Penny began to argue about putting a rug on the floor, I left the room, running to Alia's for a few moments of peace.

But Alia was sitting on her mat, trembling. Her face had turned a strange, ashen color. She looked really sick. I knew enough Arabic by now to understand that she was almost crazy with worry about her children up in the mountains. She didn't know if they were dead or alive and had no way of finding out.

I went back to the room, determined to achieve some sort of order. I couldn't live in this kind of chaos. I looked around to see what still had to be done before lockup. Everyone seemed to be involved in something. Everyone but Suzanne. She was just sitting there, listening to the gunfire.

"Suzanne," I said, "can you help me fill the thermoses while there is still water?"

She gave me a nasty look. "No, I can't. I don't want to. Do it yourself."

I felt hot anger burning inside of me. It was a terrible feeling, like a bad case of heartburn. I whirled away from Suzanne. "Jesus help me!" I couldn't stand the sight of her. I thought of *The Hiding Place* and how Corrie was good even to the evil prison guards. I wanted to be like that. I wanted to treat Suzanne with real love, no matter what she did. But I defended myself instead.

"You are my witness," I said to Chevy. "When Suzanne runs to Esther and the Paeths this time, I want them to hear the truth."

Chevy grinned. She seemed to hate Suzanne even more than I did.

"You're nothing but a dictator," Suzanne whined. Her voice rose shrilly. "I'm sick to death of you bossing me around."

I opened my mouth to tell her exactly what I thought of her. It had come to this point, and there was no return. I was shaking all over—

close to losing control. I took a few steps toward her. "Suzanne," I began. . . .

"Be quiet!"

My head snapped around. It was Anne's voice, and it meant business. "Listen—don't make a sound!" Then she began to whisper. "Do you hear something? Not the guns. Something different. There it is again."

We heard it. A faint crackling sound, coming from outside our window. "I smell something," Chevy said. We all did.

"Smoke! O dear God, it's coming in our window!"

I ran to the wall. "Quick! Somebody give me a hand, and I'll see how close it is."

Suzanne was there first. "Up you go," she said, and boosted me to the window. I fanned frantically at the smoke and tried to see. "What is it? Are we on fire?" the others cried. "What's going on?"

"I can see a roadblock . . . and, oh, there's where the smoke's coming from. Some kids have set fire to a big pile of garbage. I don't think there's any danger of it spreading, but—it's awful out there—just awful. The bombs must have been right on top of us. The streets are a mess, full of chunks of concrete and jagged glass. Lots of windows have been blown out of apartment buildings, and the doors are missing. There are big holes in the plaster walls. It looks like a cyclone came through and tore everything to pieces." I looked for another minute, taking in the rubble in the streets, the stacks of garbage which hadn't been picked up for weeks because of the fighting.

"Let me down," I told them. "I've seen enough." My voice was shaking when I spoke again. "It's war," I told them. "It's really war out there." I had heard the guns and the bombs. The noise had terrified me. But when I had looked out that window, somehow I had become involved.

By summer, conditions in our rooms grew even worse. The least little thing could set any one of us off. Arguments raged and pettiness was rampant. Finally, Mia and Percy had a fight. Not an argument this time, but a hair-pulling, face-scratching, shin-kicking brawl.

"Cut it out!" Anne shouted. "You're going to get us all in trouble!"

Mia had her hands around Percy's neck. I put my arms around Mia and tried to pull her off. Percy's legs were everywhere, kicking wildly, even at those who were trying to help her. Anne and Penny rushed in, trying to help. Suzanne and Chevy stood and screamed. There was no way to keep something like this quiet.

In a few minutes we heard Hanni's big feet thumping down the hall. She was furious—wild with anger that a thing like this could happen while she was in charge. She pushed Mia into one corner and Percy into another, shouted something at them in Arabic, and left. In a few minutes she was back with the *mudeera,* and they both stormed into the room, ordering us all out into the hallway.

Then there began a systematic search of the

corner where Chevy and Mia had their mats. "What's wrong? What are you doing to my things?" Chevy shouted at them in Arabic and finally got an answer.

Mia had tried to send an uncensored letter out by way of Esther. It contained plans to bomb her way out of here. We were all furious with Mia. "How could you do such a dumb thing? You're supposed to get your letters censored and then give them to Esther. She mails them for us, but she can't censor them. Now they won't trust her, and they won't trust us, either."

Chevy was even angrier than the rest of us, for she was being searched, and she hadn't done anything to deserve it. Hanni ignored her protests and threw Chevy's things in rumpled piles onto the floor. "Stop it!" Chevy screamed, pulling at Hanni's huge arms, scratching at her back. "You have no right. Get out of here!"

Hanni left, but not before taking all our *memnuas* with her—mirrors, scissors, pins, breakables. We would get them back in the morning, but it was an aggravation, and Hanni knew it.

By the end of the afternoon, Mia had been transferred into the room where the *sharmootas*— the prostitutes—were kept, and Chevy had been punished for resisting a search. "No prison shopping," the *mudeera* told her. "And you will be locked in room for one week."

Esther came the next day to tell us what had happened. She had gone through a regular police questioning at the prison. When she saw us, her face was pale, and her voice trembled. "I can't come here anymore," she said. "They canceled my permit because of Mia's letter."

My heart sank. What would become of us now? Esther had been so faithful, someone we could trust and count on. All our mail came through Esther. The food supplies that the kitchen girls couldn't or wouldn't get all came from Esther. I had a sick feeling of loss and dread. Little by little our contacts with the outside were becoming fewer and fewer.

I was glad to escape the depression of our room for a little while and go to Alia's where I was to sleep that night. Rahaili was leaving in the morning, and I wanted to be with her on her last night. I sat in front of her and sketched her again, intrigued by her simple elegance and strength. Ten years she had been in prison—falsely accused of murdering her husband, deprived of her children. She sang that night, a plaintive, minor song, strangely poetic. Her throaty voice rose and fell, trembling on the notes.

In the morning, she would return to her Bedouin village. And she might be in danger. There was a rumor that someone there had sworn to kill her to avenge her husband's death. It was a kind of tribal vendetta—a veiled threat—so that, even though she was innocent, she would live out her life in uncertainty, in fear.

"From one prison to another," she said. I wondered how she could seem so serene.

Later, when the lights were out, I lay on the floor listening to the gentle rhythm of Arabic voices whispering. The sound had grated on my ears a year ago, but tonight it had a musical sound.

The night sky was bright, and light came in through the window, casting deep shadows on the gray walls. I remembered how I used to feel so alone when I sat in a roomful of Arabic women. But not tonight. Tonight I felt a closeness to them—these same women whom I had once thought of as less than human. They were still poor and uneducated, and some were dirty, but I could eat and sleep with them—and laugh with them—and love them. They were, I thought, with a realization that was past surprise, my sisters.

"So, here I am, Father, a prisoner in prison. Yet so much of me is free now, that was in chains before. Thank you, Father, for what you are teaching me. Help me, I pray, to accept this experience as a gift instead of a burden."

In the morning, Rahaili dressed in a long purple dress and veil. We cried for her again, as we had the last time she left us, but this time they were tears of joy. After ten years in Sanayeh. . . Rahaili was free, and I whispered a prayer for her safety.

Rahaili was gone, but I remained. I must stay here.

And now the Paeths were coming to tell me good-bye. How I treasured the special friendship that they had offered. They had been so faithful—I had grown to depend on their support. And now they were leaving—going home.

It was dangerous for them to be out on the streets, and I hadn't known whether they could come at all. Many times they had been unable to cross the battlefront, known as no-man's land, that stretched across the city. And there was always the risk that roadblocks would go up, keeping them from returning home.

But they did come, and we sat up front together, trying to carry on a normal conversation. I gave them tapes I had made for my mother and friends. And they brought me a little mail and told me they had put some money from my father into my account. Then Jessie held out a package.

"Marti, Bob wanted you to have one last loaf of 'uncle's bread.'"

I reached out and took it. I could feel the corner of my lip begin to tremble. How could I say good-bye to them? How could I tell them how much I was going to miss them, or thank them for the way they had loved me? I didn't know what I would do when they were gone. I didn't see how I could get along without them. I tried to smile, and couldn't. I tried to talk, but a great sob rose up and filled my throat.

They understood, and they didn't try to talk anymore, either. We just sat there together until my time was up and I had to go. "Marti, will you send Suzanne up so we can say good-bye to her, too?"

I called Suzanne, then stood alone in the hallway. I wanted desperately to run back—back to the visitors' room to see them one more time. But I couldn't. Suzanne was there. I felt so abandoned. So alone. With tears streaming down my face, I walked through the corridor to the courtyard door. Someone had left it unlocked. I pushed it open and stepped out. I could hear the guns beyond the wall, and the bombs exploding in the distance. But in the courtyard the sun was shining. I sat on the steps and lifted my face.

"Come, Father, and take away this loneliness. Help me cope with the loss of my friends."

It was then that I felt his presence, as warm as the sun against my skin, and far more comforting. The icy frustration I had felt deep inside me began to melt, and I could feel myself warming all the way through. How good it felt!

CHAPTER

22

"Please, leave the door unlocked," I pleaded with the guard. "Please!"

"No!" the guard snapped. "Will be locked in every day now."

Every day! "Oh, no, Father. Don't let them lock us in every day. I can't stand it in this tiny little room with the door closed."

I began to cry. "Please, go ask the *mudeera*. Please!"

Suddenly, like an answer to my prayer, the *mudeera* came stalking down the hall, entered our room, and ordered Madame Chevalier moved to another room. "Now you be unlocked as usual," she said.

I was so grateful I didn't even complain when three new girls were herded into the room with us. Percy was leaving and Chevy had moved, so it really didn't make any difference. I dried my eyes and fixed them something to eat. In order for them to have any bedding, the sheeting that divided the room would have to come down. That would mean no more divided areas. I didn't even hesitate, but pulled it all down and handed it over. From now on, we would have an open room.

The hot days were upon us, and we were often without water. The bombs had broken the water mains, and repairs were patchy and never permanent. The water supply would be cut off for hours—even days at a time, and there wouldn't be a drop to drink. We even begged for the dirty water from the guards' room. It was full of straw and dirt, but we thought we could put purifying pills in it, then boil it and use it. Sometimes we had to try to get clean by sponging our bodies with a little rubbing alcohol.

Adding to our discomfort was the foul stench that came from the *loo*. We tried to save our leftover wash water to flush it, but we never had enough to do much good.

When water did come, it was early in the morning, long before anyone was awake. It would run for a while, then stop. If we missed it, we were dry for at least another day.

At night, we tried keeping the taps open, with a bucket underneath, so that, hopefully, someone would hear the dribbling sound and wake up.

Sanayeh was like a desert, where water was more precious than food or gold. When we had water, we felt rich; we felt blessed. Water meant survival.

One morning, I was lying on my mat, not

awake, yet not quite sleeping. I didn't want to wake up yet. It was too early. I wanted to drift away into pleasant dreams of another time—another place.

Marti. It's time to get up. . . .

A thought came, like a gentle tap on my shoulder. But it wasn't time to get up. I closed my eyes tighter. *Marti.* This time it was a nudge. I opened my eyes and listened. Water! I distinctly heard the sound of running water. I jumped up from my mat and filled all our buckets, thermoses, and kettles right up to the rim. When I finished, the water was still running, so I stripped off my nightclothes and took a cold shower, washed my hair, then scrubbed out my clothes and bedding. Water, blessed water! Oh, how wonderful it felt to be clean again. I even took one of the overflowing buckets and threw it down the terrible *loo.* It gurgled and sloshed, then flushed with a loud noise like a cough. All the accumulated filth disappeared. I felt like clapping my hands, but grabbed the empty bucket and refilled it instead.

Suddenly, without warning, the pressure dropped. In a few minutes, there was only a thin stream. By daylight, when the rest of the prison was awake, the water had stopped running altogether. There wasn't another drop for the rest of the day.

Often, after that, I would awaken in the night or early in the morning to the same gentle touch, like a loving tap on my shoulder. And I would hear the sound of running water. Then I stumbled out of bed and filled the buckets and offered a grateful prayer. "Thank you, Father. Thank you for waking me in time."

On dry days, whenever we were unlocked, we would roam the prison searching for water, carrying buckets and each going in a different direction. We would try the kitchen, the other bathrooms, the offices, then finally the guards' room. The guards' room almost always had water, but it was off limits, and we weren't supposed to go near it. We always approached cautiously to see who was there. If Noha were on duty, she would give us some water, but Hanni would shout and shake her fists and chase us away.

One morning, when I was up early, I discovered that there wasn't even a trickle. The day was already hot, and I knew that without any water at all we would feel mean and miserable by midmorning. I got unlocked to go to the kitchen, but there was not water there, either.

The halls were empty. Not a guard in sight. I tiptoed to the forbidden guards' room and stood listening at the door. Someone was in there, snoring loudly. I peeked in and saw Hanni, lying on her back with her mouth wide open. Just beyond her was the faucet, and I could see water slowly dripping from the tap. My mouth felt dry—drier. I took a few steps forward. She didn't move. Cautiously I slipped across the floor, past Hanni's bed, and filled my kettle. Hanni slept on. I ran back to the room, grabbed a bucket in each hand, and returned. Two more trips past the slumbering giant and we had water for another day. What would she have done, I wondered, if she had caught me?

In July, a new government was formed, and the fighting temporarily stopped. The main pipes were repaired, and we celebrated by taking three and four showers a day. I stood beneath the cool water letting myself imagine that it was washing all my worries down the drain, giving thanks all the while for the abundance of the Lord's blessings. The mains could be bombed out tomorrow, and we would again live in a dry prison world. But I couldn't think about that now. I didn't let myself think about tomorrow. Today was all I could manage.

One day at a time, Marti. One day at a time.

Abruptly, another girl was thrust into our room. She had just been released from the prison hospital and was still on medication. She looked like a fat zombie, and her speech was so slurred that it was almost incomprehensible. She drooled from the corners of her mouth, which always hung open.

Wait a minute—there was something familiar— I looked at her closer. "Oh, no!" I exclaimed in horror. This grotesque basket case was Bridget— the hardened, overconfident pro who had been with us for one night in April. We had all been so impressed with her self-confidence and daring. I remembered how I had said a prayer for her. What could have happened to her to make her like this?

We never found out. Jan, one of the new arrivals who said she had been a nurse, took over much of Bridget's care. She dressed her in the morning and undressed her at night. At mealtimes she had to feed her like a baby. Sometimes I asked her to eat with Anne and Penny and me, and even though it was worse to watch her eat than it was Suzanne, I felt as though I was being given a second chance—an opportunity to show love to someone who was so unlovable.

Tension mounted as more new girls came in and we had to find room for them, too. Outside, the bombing began again, the mains broke, and we had no water at all. The stench from the *loo* was unbearable. We all began to fear disease from the lack of sanitation in a hot Middle-Eastern summer. One of the girls wet her bed at night and never washed her sheets, and the pungent smell of urine was sickening. Because one of the Arab prisoners had tried to escape, the courtyard was locked and we couldn't get outside. We couldn't enjoy the early morning sun or feel the coolness of an occasional breeze. We lived in a crowded, smoke-filled room—hot, airless, suffocating. No wonder life seemed unbearable for all of us.

And for me—there was always the ever-present Suzanne.

I started reading the *Love Book* for the third time and was struck by a verse.

If any one says, "I love God," and hates his brother, he is a liar; for he who does not love his brother whom he has seen, cannot love God whom he has not seen (1 John 4:20 RSV).

Even then I could not bring myself to like Suzanne. I managed to stop picking at her, but there was no love in my heart for her. And, try as I might, I couldn't even ignore her.

I was horrified when Anne and Penny warned me that I was beginning to make faces—odd, twisted faces—when I was reading or sitting quietly, trying to think. My voice, they told me, was getting high and shrill.

Like Suzanne's? "Oh, Father, don't let me whine like that. Don't let me be like her!"

And then I remembered the Pharisee who had been so thankful he wasn't like other men. The proud Pharisee. Proud like me.

But I know I'm not like her. Not at all. Am I?

God's children, Marti. You are all God's children.

I couldn't sleep that night. Sweat dripped down my back and soaked my hair. I tossed and turned, unable to stop my mind from churning. All the hateful things that Suzanne had done to me popped up like cardboard scenes on a puppet stage. One by one, I reviewed them, savoring them in my mind. I really wanted to have loving feelings toward her. I knew I needed to forgive her. But I just couldn't. How could I when she was so vicious and spiteful and mean—a "filthy savage," just like Chevy said. I'm not like that. I know I'm not!

Think about it, Marti.

I didn't want to think about it. I wanted somebody to give me some answers I could live with. I had wanted so much out of life, and now I had so little. Why . . . why? I picked up one of my books and read something by C. S. Lewis. I read it carefully and then reread it. "God intends to give us what we need, not what we now think we want."

Did this mean that I was getting what I needed, and that getting out of prison would not make me happy? How could anyone need an experience like this? I didn't understand. I just didn't understand. But I did know that if it were true, it would be a bitter pill to swallow.

By this time, most of the girls were taking tranquilizers regularly, and sometimes I was tempted to join them. Those were the days when I turned to the *Love Book* for comfort. "Give me strength, Father," I would pray.

And he did, even on the day when I was tempted most. For suddenly, without a word of warning, Chevy was back. She just walked in one morning in September, dropped her bedding, and ran to the office to demand her old corner space back. She looked different to me, somehow—like an old, broken woman struggling to cope, just like the rest of us were. I was determined not to treat her badly, as I still grieved over the way I had tried to barricade her with sheets. While she was gone, we gathered up her bedding and put her in a good spot in the corner. When she returned, she looked around in surprise, then shrugged and began to quietly put her things away.

The next morning, I heard the courtyard gate being unlocked far earlier than usual. Our door was unlocked, too, and I ran out in my nightgown to see what was going on. The Arabs in two of the rooms were dragging their storage cupboards down the hallway and out into the courtyard. They had emptied everything out of them so that they were completely bare. One of the women wrapped old rags around a long stick, lit it like a Roman torch, and passed the flame over the cabinets, inside and outside, charring the wood and letting a little of it catch fire. Masses of black cockroaches fled from the cupboards swarming over the ground, running all over the yard like wild things.

I picked up the hem of my nightgown and jumped up on a bench to escape them—a river of black shiny bodies crawling beneath me. The roach hunt lasted all morning. I couldn't help wondering where they would all go. I found out soon enough. They hid in our food, in the cracks in our walls, and in the *loo*.

But I didn't have time to worry about things like roaches when the shooting was getting so much worse. We could hear it right outside the walls—rapid bursts of gunfire, followed by screaming voices. A big bomb exploded near the prison, and we were locked in all day. A little water was brought into the prison—only enough to wet our mouths and none at all for washing.

That night the *mudeera* marched through the corridors telling all prisoners to put out their lights. "There is much fighting in the streets," she said. "Even one candle is forbidden." One by one, the lights went out, and we sat in total darkness. Outside, sirens wailed. Whistles blew. Now and then someone would scream. Another burst of gunfire. Silence. No one in the prison tried to sleep.

Shopping became dangerous for all in Beirut, and food supplies were scarce. An old man came each week and brought us what he could, but the food was bad and old, and the prices were higher than our limited funds could afford. Penny became a master at making miracle meals from bits and scraps for me, Anne, and herself. We didn't complain, for we were lucky to eat at all.

And we were lucky to survive the wrath of the kitchen girls when we tried to cook. The war was getting on their nerves, too, and they took it out on us by screaming and cursing. Most of them were in prison for killing their husbands, and we tried to stay out of their way, especially when they were wielding knives.

Once, at the end of September, we heard the news on a little radio that we kept hidden in the room. "No more shooting," the announcement said. "All prisoners will be released." But we had heard that same old story many times before, and nothing ever happened. It was what we called a "Lebanese promise." A little less than maybe.

"Ma fi shey! Ma fi shey!" ("Nothing! Nothing!") October started off as our nothing month. No water, no gas for the stove, no food, no Esther, no Paeths, no mail, no money. Nothing. *Ma fi shey!* I started praying hard and fast!

Outside, the war raged on, and we listened nervously to the hidden radio in our room, waiting daily to get our news from the BBC.

Beirut's oldest marketplace, the *Souk Sursock,* was reduced to rubble by bombs—400 mortar shells fell on one area in a single day—over 500 shops have been destroyed, adding to the food shortages—2,800 people have been killed in the fighting since April—once beautiful Beirut is now little more than a scarred battlefield.

Unexpectedly, an answer came to some of our prayers. The British Embassy managed to get some money into Anne's and Penny's accounts, and David King, Bob Paeth's friend, got through with some money for me. We were able to order a little food again.

But by the next Saturday, the fighting had intensified, and thunder and rain added to the darkness of the day. The little money that David had put into my account was already gone; we were completely out of food. With the battles going on outside, no one would even try to get through to us again. Would God answer my prayers for provisions again—not just for me, but for all of us?

God did. Norman Horner, Esther's husband, took a terrible chance and made his way through the bombed-out streets to the prison. "Things are getting worse," he told me. "Most of the shops and banks are closed. People are forced to buy on credit at the few shops that are still open." He handed me some letters, a box of food, and a receipt for some extra money he had just deposited in my prison account.

For a few days, we felt safer, but the food was

soon eaten, and the money was spent. Our only hope was for amnesty. But I knew that Mary Mathias had escaped, as had most private citizens, to seek refuge in the mountains. The courts were closed because of the fighting. How would any of us manage to get out?

The *mudeera* began compiling a list of names to submit to a special committee. "Monday," she told us. "I will put in papers to committee on Monday. Within ten days you will surely have amnesty." She nodded confidently. "Not to worry," she assured us.

We had heard it all before. The "Lebanese promise." "Not to worry—not to worry." And then nothing was ever done. Serving out the entire sentence of three years or being killed by a stray bomb seemed to be a real possibility for all of us.

"Heavenly Father," I prayed, "please release me. I know you can. You're the only one who can."

The fighting outside was always reflected by increased fighting inside, and now it was worse than ever. The guards yelled at the prisoners and tried to lock us in our rooms for days at a time. The Arabs screamed back at the guards, shouting hate-filled messages. And they they screamed at us, wishing we could understand.

We did not scream in the room like the Arabs did because we were too "civilized." But the tension was as bad as if we had. Our voices became tense and controlled and we made petty accusations of each other, putting blame where no blame lay. And I was as bad as any of the

others. Even though I tried hard to be patient—
to stay calm—my control often slipped, and my
temper flared.

One day when it was my turn to clean the *loo,*
I went to get a plastic bag for the bathroom
trash. I couldn't find any on the communal shelf
where they were supposed to be.

"The bags are gone!" I shouted. "Which one
of you took them?" I looked directly at Mia. She
was always such a pack rat—picking up scraps
of things and storing them away in her boxes.
"Where are they, Mia? I know you have them!"

Anne gave me a troubled look and walked
over to the shelf. She searched around for a
minute and pulled out the package of bags. They
had been there all the time, pushed to the back—
right where I had put them.

The room was strangely silent. I could feel
them all watching me. "How could you, Marti?"
Chevy finally asked. Her usually harsh voice was
quiet, subdued. "How could you accuse someone so quickly when it was your own mistake . . .
your own forgetfulness?"

How could I indeed? I felt grieved and humbled and said so, asking Mia to forgive me. But I
did it again. It was because one of my precious
eggs was missing. Someone had to have stolen it.
It sure didn't get up and walk away by itself.

Madame Chevalier loved eggs. She was always
begging for one, never seeming to have enough.
She was the obvious culprit, I decided. Stealing
was right down her line. I confronted her with
my suspicions and asked her a blunt question.
"Chevy, did you steal one of my eggs?"

She was furious, outraged. Her face turned purple, and she refused to answer me at all. "Wait a minute, Marti," Anne said. "Don't you remember? You gave an egg to one of the Arab girls yesterday morning."

I looked at Chevy's angry face and felt sick inside. "Chevy, I'm sorry. I'm really sorry," I began. "Please forgive me. I didn't mean. . . ."

"Yes, you did," she stormed. "You meant exactly what you said. That's the trouble with you, Marti. You think you're better than any of us. It doesn't bother you to make other people look small, because you think we're already small—smaller than you. Marti the Great! Marti the Magnificent! You think you're so pure, Marti, but I'm going to tell you the truth. You're the worst one of all, and you don't even know it."

Her words stung. I tried to close my ears. I didn't want to listen. But Chevy had painted a picture of me that I couldn't avoid looking at. It was an ugly picture that humbled and shamed me. Marti the Pharisee, I thought, who rejoices that she is not like other men. . . .

CHAPTER
23

The dark, cold months of another winter were
upon us. I developed a severe ear infection and
lay for days at a time upon my mat, holding my
pillow tightly against my head, trying not to cry
with the pain. The terrible depression that we
called the "Sanayeh Blues" spread through our
room like a highly contagious disease. The very
air seemed gray and dull, and our thoughts were
on survival as we scrounged for food and tried
desperately to keep warm.

Our hidden radio brought bad news:

Heavy fighting by the big hotels—American
Embassy closed—hundreds of armed men
roaming the streets—

As the sounds of bombs and shooting continued, ever closer, the Egyptian women got
hysterical and banged on their doors and

270

screamed, "Send us home! Send us back to Egypt!"

The *mudeera* stormed through the prison with all the available soldiers she could muster. She screamed. The Arab women screamed back. The bombs fell. My ear throbbed.

Anne and Penny went to the *mudeera* to ask about the amnesty papers she had promised to file. She only gave them a blank look, shook her head, and mumbled, "Later! Later! Too many troubles now."

Thanksgiving came and went, and Christmas was approaching. It was a cold, cold winter, with howling winds and bitter rains. David and Maxine King wrote a short note:

> *We tried to visit you, but fighting broke out and caused unbelievable traffic jams. It was too dangerous to be out on the streets. At least eighty people were killed. They are already calling it Black Saturday!*

I didn't think much about amnesty anymore. My eighteen months were up in December—on Christmas day. But who knew what December would bring?

I continued waking up early each morning, as I had for many months now. I would open my eyes slowly—so slowly. I was alive. I would decide that I had been given another day to live. And I was thankful. Not for a great occasion— not for something that had happened in the past or might happen in the future. I was grateful for this single moment in time. This *now*. I felt a peace inside of me that had nothing to do with what was happening around me. But today was all I could manage, and I took it gladly.

"The rest is yours, Lord."

It always was, Marti. It always was.

By this time I had a certain routine to my day that filled my hours, and I felt that I was using my time constructively. But the things that Chevy had said to me still lay heavily on my mind. "Marti the Great—Marti the Magnificent." I thought again of the way I had treated people I didn't like—of the way I had hurt people I loved—of relationships I wished I could forget. I had been moody, aloof, selfish, rigid, compulsive, bossy, and I was a liar. How I wished I could erase the hurts I had caused in the past!

Then open your heart, Marti, and let me change you some more.

Tears filled my eyes and I wanted to scream with rage—"but it's not so easy. I don't know how! I don't know how to start!"

Suddenly I remembered a verse from Isaiah:

Thus says the Lord . . . "Remember not the former things, nor consider the things of old. Behold, I am doing a new thing, now it springs forth, do you not perceive it?" (Isaiah 43:16–19, RSV).

You can start with today, Marti. You have today. Why don't you use it?

Was it that simple? Suddenly the gray winter air seemed to clear around me. I had today and I could use it. That meant doing something with it. Something concrete to erase the past. It was the "new thing" that was important—"even now it is springing to light."

I looked across the room at Chevy and remembered the look on her face that awful day when I had hung the sheets around her. She was gathering her mat now, rolling it up so she could carry it outside to air it. I rolled mine, too, and followed her to the courtyard.

"Chevy," I said, "do you remember when I said those mean things to you and sewed your sheet up?"

She looked at me suspiciously. "I remember."

"Well," my voice was trembling, and I felt close to tears. "Well, I'm so sorry for that. Chevy, do you think that . . . that you can ever forgive me?"

She stared at me. There was a sudden warmth in her eyes that touched me. Then, unexpectedly, she began to laugh. "Marti, don't think about it anymore. If I were to carry around resentments over things like that, I would just make myself sick. I have enough burdens, Marti, without that one!"

We sat together quietly in the sun, warming ourselves. "It's nice out here in the mornings," I said. "At least as nice as it can be in prison."

Chevy nodded. "It's nicer when you have friends."

A little later, I took a piece of paper and wrote a note to Esther. "Please forgive me," I said, "for all the complications and worries I've caused you and for the ways that I've tried to excuse and justify myself instead of admitting I was wrong."

"There," I thought. "Now I've done all I can." But it wasn't enough. One day I picked up a copy of *My Daily Bread* and read, "Those who think it is permissible to tell white lies soon go color-blind."

That couldn't be true, could it? Little white lies were a means to an end. I had used them for years . . . in my life at home, with Jim, at The Bridge, with Dimitri. . . .

That's the trouble, Marti. Your life is a pattern of lies.

A pattern of lies? If that were true, then my life in prison was the biggest lie of all. For I was guilty. As guilty as any of the others. And I had lied about my guilt to the people I loved the most.

There was only one thing I could do to rid myself of the sickness I felt inside of me.

I began to tell the truth. The whole truth—not the little bits and pieces that had started years and years ago and had grown into the giant lie that was my life. I wrote to my mother and my friends at home and told them that I was guilty. Guilty as charged. Every bit as guilty as Dimitri. I asked them to forgive me . . . and I hoped that they could someday forget. . . .

And then I did the most important thing of all. I asked the Lord to forgive me for living a lie. It was such a big thing to ask forgiveness for, but all I could think of was a simple prayer. "Lord, forgive me for being a liar. Give me the courage to tell the truth.''

I should have felt better. I wanted to feel better. But there was still Suzanne. I could not bring myself to talk to her. I wanted to say I was sorry, but I wasn't. She kept doing things to irritate and hurt me, and I couldn't have the same warm feelings toward her that I had toward the others. ''Forgive me, Father. I can't find it in my heart to love her.''

But how do you treat her?

How do I treat her? What difference did that make? It was my feelings that counted.

And your actions.

My actions? What good were actions without feelings? Was this what God wanted? For me to pretend—to treat that little crybaby with kindness? Well, I couldn't do it. I couldn't!

Yes, you can, Marti. Even if you can't feel loving, you can be loving.

I bit my lip. It was true. I wondered if Christ felt loving when he died on the cross. No matter. He went ahead and did a loving act. Even if I didn't feel loving toward Suzanne, I could be kind. But I . . . I just didn't know how to start. ''Oh, Father, what is it you want of me? What do you expect me to do?''

Start small, Marti. Start with small acts of kindness.

I tried to tell myself I had already done all I could. I wasn't strong enough to do any more. After all, Suzanne was to blame, too. I tried to put Suzanne clear out of my mind, but I couldn't.

275

She kept popping up like unfinished business, and I knew I was going to have to do something about her. "Help me, Father. Help me find a way."

One day, I noticed Suzanne poking around her messy side of the room making a halfhearted attempt to clean it up, and I offered to help. It was a major project, involving even her mat and all her boxes. It would have been easy to criticize, and there were plenty of opportunities. "Help me, Father, to keep my thoughts to myself. Give me the strength to get through this one act of kindess." The Lord listened, and I managed to keep my mouth shut.

A little later we worked together organizing the "library"—the piles of books that had accumulated in the foreigners' section of the prison. I had to admit that Suzanne could be organized when she was interested in what she was doing. But an efficient Suzanne was not something I had grown to expect, so I was not surprised to see that as soon as she lost interest, she reverted to her old messy ways. "Give me patience, Lord. Let me be understanding." We completed sorting the books, and it went better than I expected . . . with a lot of help from the Lord.

Then I began to notice another woman in the prison—one of the newcomers whose name was Amena. She was Jewish and had been arrested for spying. This didn't mean that she was guilty—only that she was Jewish, and therefore an object of hate. The feeling against Jews in some quarters was harsh—even fierce. I remembered

Jessie Paeth telling me about one girl who was tortured because she had gone sightseeing to Israel. A Star of David with the word "Jew" had been carved on her body, and the pain and shock had left her unconscious.

Perhaps Amena was lucky to have been just imprisoned. But because the prison was largely Arabic, she was ostracized and ridiculed until she stayed apart from the other prisoners, eating and sleeping without speaking to anyone. She had always looked so scruffy and dirty that I had ignored her, but now I began to watch her, seeing something about her that reminded me of Suzanne. Neither of them had very high standards of cleanliness, but I didn't hate Amena for that, the way I had hated Suzanne.

Why? Because I was trying to accept Suzanne. Was it easier for me to accept someone else whom I would have formerly looked down upon? By showing acts of kindness to Suzanne, was I finding it easier to have loving feelings toward others who seemed unlovable?

Oh, how the Lord does work in mysterious ways! How patiently he works within me to open up my heart.

So I sat with Amena and talked to her and even loaned her some of my precious books to read. She was a surprisingly well-educated woman, I discovered, and she had a pleasant, kind way about her that made me ashamed of the way I had once felt. One day she presented me with a pair of warm slippers that she had knitted, and I cut and styled her hair in return.

See, Marti? Do you see what I am doing?

277

When letters came from home saying, "Marti, we felt you were guilty and we loved you just the same," they made me feel cherished. But I was, I told myself, so undeserving of their love and trust, for I had been so wrong. To show my appreciation for friends back home—for their faithfulness and kindness—I spent a month creating for each one a handmade Christmas card, with hand-painted pictures and special quotes from my readings. Then I made Christmas cards and little gifts for each woman in the room and for Alia. The work was a blessing—an unexpected therapy—for I spent those days before Christmas thinking of others rather than myself.

We all wondered what Christmas would be like this year without Esther—without the Paeths—with the war still raging on. I awoke early on Christmas day and tiptoed around the crowded room to put my tiny gift beside each mat. I couldn't help remembering how I had felt the year before, depressed and angry and dependent on little white pills to keep me from feeling or thinking. Even with things as bad as they were, this year seemed to me to be better than last, for there was joy in my heart and a wondrous feeling of awe that I could experience peace in the midst of the turmoil around us.

We all knew there would be no dinner. It was impossible because of the war. And I knew I would have no visitors. Esther was gone; the Paeths were gone; Mary Mathias was in the mountains. So I was as surprised as anyone when a visitor's call came for me. I ran up front to see who it could be and found—not a visitor at all—but unexpectedly, miraculously, a feast!

We never knew who brought it, for the box said simply, "Merry Christmas!" There were ten chickens, three boxes of pastries, a box of apples, a box of oranges, hot mashed potatoes, gravy, rolls, and even candy bars—one for each girl.

Even though it was bitterly cold, we rolled up our mats and had a party, sharing the food with Alia and even with the guards. The Lord had provided. We had reason to celebrate!

After Christmas, I heard from the embassy. "Your paperwork is sorted, and you will be going home soon." I took a deep breath and let it out slowly. By the first of the year—only a few short days away. Soon I would be breathing the air of freedom, I thought.

But the first of the year dragged by. It was January 1976, and there was no further word of my release. I knew that my amnesty papers were on the president's desk. They needed only to be signed. A mere formality was keeping me from getting out of this place and going home. That— and a raging war. "Oh, Father, give me courage, and patience, and hope. And could you please also get me out of here!"

The BBC did nothing to cheer us up. According to the news, the fighting was reaching its peak; 4,500 establishments had been destroyed by fire or rockets. The now constant fires threatened to destroy the prison along with the rest of the city.

Suddenly, on January 6, things began to happen. A note came from Mary Mathias. "Dear Marti," it said, "please sign this paper I've prepared for your amnesty."

She hadn't forgotten me! Even while she was hiding in the mountains, she had managed to remember to do all the necessary things! I remembered that day long ago when she had scolded me for not trusting her, and I felt ashamed. It occurred to me that I hadn't trusted God, either, and I felt doubly ashamed.

A similar note arrived from my embassy. "Miss Sinclair, your lawyer has prepared papers for your amnesty, and we look forward to your release."

Did this mean that my amnesty had actually been signed at last? My father had sent money to the embassy for my ticket. Everything seemed to be all set. All I had to do now, I told myself, was wait. I walked in a daze, packing my clothes and books, unable to believe that this was happening. Daily, I expected to be called up front. It was as Mary told me so long ago, "just a matter of time, Marti—just a matter of time."

But no one called me. I waited a week, and there was nothing. Then one day Norman was able to get through. He brought donuts and cheese for all of us and a letter for me. It was from my father and was dated November 26, 1976. "Dear Marti, plans are all made and confirmed, and we're eagerly awaiting your arrival home on January 9."

Yesterday!

I cried in my room the rest of the day. I was going to spend the whole three years of my sentence in this rotten place. We all were. And there wasn't one blessed thing we could do about it. "Father, why the delay?"

I unpacked my books and put them back by my mat. I tried to go on with my usual daily routine. And I began to read again: Paul Tournier, Catherine Marshall, Francis Schaeffer. I began to take a good look at myself—to see myself as I had once been and as I now was. I began to realize that past wrongs—and daily wrongs here in the prison—had to be brought up and confessed. They were short-circuiting my relationship with my Father. They had to be looked at squarely and confessed before the Lord could forgive me or answer my prayers.

I thought of the way I had lived, and all my sexual experiences came to mind. It had started so long ago, way back when I was eighteen. I remembered each situation, each man, the relationships I had enjoyed, and the relationships I regretted. One by one I brought them to mind until I saw them vividly. Then I asked forgiveness, and I asked God to let me forgive myself.

At the end, when I remembered Dimitri, I said once again, "I'm sorry, Lord. Forgive me," and then, "He was the last, Lord. There will be no more until you choose someone for me."

I prayed hard that night. I prayed for the will and courage to save myself—to wait for marriage and to remember that the more special a thing is, the more it should be set aside and saved for a special time and a very special person.

The next day I told Anne and Penny and they

laughed. "You're kidding!" they exclaimed. "You mean no more sex—ever—until you're married?"

There were very few secrets among the three of us. We had shared confidences, and they knew me well—the way I had lived with Dimitri, and those before him.

"Oh, Marti!" they giggled. "You'll never be able to hold out. It's OK in here where there aren't any men, but wait until you get on the outside. You'll see!"

It hurt to be laughed at, for I knew they didn't believe me, and there was no way I could make them understand. They knew I couldn't do it, and I knew I could.

Something was happening inside of me. I couldn't explain it, but it must have shown, for one day I received a letter from Esther:

Marti, I sense that something big has happened to you. There is no more hardness about your eyes—just a beauty you didn't have a year ago. Even your physical carriage has changed. You seem calm and serene—quite different from before, and I do believe your life will be different from now on. There is a peace and tranquility in your heart now. Yes?

But there was still something wrong with my heart, for I was not completely content. I still resented the delay. Hadn't I learned all the lessons I needed to learn? Wasn't I doing what the Lord asked me, by showing acts of kindness? Wasn't I trying as hard as I could? If only God could show me that there was a purpose in all of this. If only I could have some plain, honest answers. "Father, why do I need to stay in prison longer? It's time for me to go home."

I felt restless, agitated, and went out into the hall to rummage through the boxes, looking for a book I hadn't read. I picked up one, and then another, discarding them as worthless, dull, or just not what I wanted. Then my fingers closed around a paperback book, and I pulled a New Testament out of the box.

Something held me, and I opened the cover, flipping idly through the pages. The book was old and worn, with dog-eared leaves, as if someone had turned them again and again. I began to read, without any purpose, just letting my eyes wander down the pages, going from verse to verse, page to page. I felt the same rhythm, the same sense of gentle music that I had found in the *Love Book*.

I stopped turning pages. I was in the book of Luke, and one verse caught my eye: "If you love those who love you, what credit is that to you?" A shiver went down my spine, and I moved my eyes up the page and stopped again. "Love your enemies, do good to those who hate you. . . ."

I closed the book and went into the room and sat down on my mat. "I don't love Suzanne, Lord. Most of the time I don't even like her. But I have been doing as you asked. I have tried to show her acts of kindness. Isn't that enough?"

Have you asked for her forgiveness? If you want to love your enemies, you must forgive those who hate you.

It was asking too much . . . too much. It was more than I could bear. I had asked for peace, and the prison was still filled with confusion. I had prayed for patience, and the Lord put me with people who made patience impossible.

Suddenly I remembered something that the Kings had given me on their last visit. I took my New Testament with me, went back to my bed, found the piece of paper, and read it.

God puts his own with the people and in the place which will tend most to develop spiritual graces. He puts one who is quick with one who is slow, and one who is quiet with one who is talkative; that the one who is quick may be patient with the one who is slow, and the one who is quiet may be patient with the one who is talkative. He puts one who is orderly with one who is untidy, that both may learn lessons. Often our environment is but an answer to our prayers.

My hands were shaking when I read it again. So this was what it was all about! There was a purpose, after all. There was a reason for what I had been through. All these long, miserable days in prison had value. I felt a peace that I had not felt before. For although I didn't know what the future held, I knew who held the future. I had looked for God desperately and had not found him. But even as I was looking, he had found me. I leaned my head back and closed my eyes.

I was through—finished. I wouldn't fight him anymore. "You win," I whispered. "I give up. If you want me to stay here and finish out my sentence—then I accept that. You decide. Do what you want, and not what I want. I put myself in your hands. I give you carte blanche with the rest of my life. Not my will, but yours, Lord, be done."

I sat there awhile, amazed! I had just done what I had feared to do for years. The thing I thought I could never say, I had said. And instead of feeling miserable and boxed in by God, I felt contented and hopeful. I felt loved—really loved for the first time in my life.

I knew, though, that there was still a piece of unfinished business for me to take care of. I got up with a sigh and took a pen and piece of paper from one of my boxes.

"Dear Suzanne," I wrote. "Please forgive me for the hateful way I have treated you. If you are ever in San Francisco, I hope you will visit me." I added my address and telephone number, and I took the paper and put it on her mat.

The very next evening she sent me a note saying that it was she who really owed me forgiveness and telling me how grateful she was that I had written. As I stood there, reading her words for the second time, my resentment toward her seemed to evaporate, drying up like little drops of water on a hot stove—until finally there was no hatred, no pettiness, no antagonism left—only a warm, comfortable feeling deep inside me.

Praise God, I was free! No matter what date was set by the Lebanese courts—*this* day was my release date. I was free at last!

CHAPTER

24

The news report on BBC announced in early March that the inmates of the men's prisons had been released. Our hopes soared, at first. But we heard nothing more about our situation, and the days dragged slowly on.

On March 16, I awoke, as usual, very early in the morning. It was generally quiet at this hour, but today I could hear voices out in the hall as the Arab prisoners called back and forth to each other, and the guards jabbered excitedly.

When I went to the little hatch in the door and called out my daily, *"Iftahi al-bab!"* ("Unlock the door!") the guard flatly refused.

"La!" she said firmly and shook her head from side to side.

"Please," I persisted. *"Min fadlik . . . iftahi al-bab."*

When she saw that I wasn't going to give up easily, she shrugged and unlocked the door just long enough for me to run to the kitchen and grab a couple of eggs and some lettuce. I glanced quickly out through the wire-covered kitchen window and saw soldiers marching back and forth. They were carrying machine guns, and so were the guards that stood on the rooftops all around Sanayeh. I hurried back to our room to cook my eggs on the hot plate.

The halls were full of guards, standing around in small groups and talking noisily. I kept hearing the same word repeated over and over in excited tones: *"'afu!"* ("amnesty!"). But I had been hearing that for the past six months, and nothing had happened yet. I wouldn't get excited, I told myself. I would believe it when they let me walk through the front door. In the meantime, I was going to cook my eggs and eat my breakfast.

The guard unlocked the door to the room to put me back in, and I was almost stampeded by the girls who burst past me into the hall. They had heard the voices, too, and they all knew by now what *'afu* meant. They were determined to get their suitcases from the stack in the hall, and there was nothing the guard could do to stop them.

"Come on, Marti," Penny urged me. "Hurry up and get packed. Don't you want to be ready to go?"

I shrugged and put my eggs into the boiling water. "It's probably just another false alarm."

"OK, but your suitcase is the only one left out there in the hall."

I had to laugh. I couldn't have gotten it into the room now if I had tried. The floor was covered with mats, moving bodies, clothes, and the contents of bedside boxes. The girls were packing as rapidly as they could, stuffing some things into their suitcases, thrusting others aside. The room had been crowded before; now it was impossible. My suitcase, I thought, would have been the last straw. I calmly cracked my eggs, ate my breakfast, and watched them. After all this was over, they were just going to have to unpack again.

Late that afternoon, I still hadn't brought my suitcase in. Why should I? Nothing was happening. I was starting to eat some salad when I heard a noise down the hall. Voices—footsteps—and then the soldiers appeared, surging into the corridors, peering into each room. They stalked up and down with their machine guns over their shoulders, acting as if they were looking for something—or someone.

Anne nudged me. "Marti, those aren't Lebanese soldiers, are they?"

I shook my head. They wore green uniforms and red berets. Everything about them was neat and trim. "I think," Mia told us, "that they're from the Syrian Army."

"No," Penny said. "They look like the PLA to me."

Whoever they were, we watched them silently. Why were they here? What did they want? There was a feeling of expectancy in the air, like a pause before the end of a sentence. Suddenly, one of the Arab girls started banging on her door and screaming. It seemed almost like a signal, for the prison erupted into sound. Women yelled in all their languages and dialects. "We want out! We want out!"

The *mudeera* came running out of her office and down the hallway. She was in her housecoat, pulling it tightly around her. *"Shu bike?—* What's the matter with you?" she demanded. "Be quiet! Everyone will be all right. As soon as we get our orders, we will let you go."

The screaming diminished, but there was still an excited clatter, punctuated by nervous laughter. When she came down by the foreigners' rooms, she stopped and told us not to worry. "The armed guards will escort each of you to your embassy as soon as you are released. Not to worry—not to worry."

Her promises may have calmed the Arabs, but we had been hearing her lies and "Lebanese promises" for months. I watched through the doorway as the soldiers continued prowling the hall, looking in one room and then another. "They aren't just sightseeing," I whispered to Anne. "They're after something. What do you suppose they want?"

There was a sudden commotion in one of the other rooms, the sound of a man's angry voice, a woman protesting.

"No!" she kept saying. Over and over. "No . . . no . . . no!"

They brought her out into the hallway. I saw her pull back and try to wrench herself free. Two of the soldiers grabbed her by the arms and swung her around so that she was facing me.

It was Amena—the Jewish woman I had grown to like. *Amena.* My lips formed her name, but no sound came out. Her eyes caught mine, held them. I could see the fear, the distress on her face. She was trying so hard to keep herself under control. I saw her draw herself erect, lift her chin, bite her lip to keep it from trembling. But the men pulled her hands roughly behind her back and wrapped heavy cord around her wrists. Then one of them took a dirty cloth and tied it over her eyes.

"Amena!" I called her name and saw her head move in response. One of the men glanced in my direction, took a few steps forward.

"Stay out of it, Marti." It was Chevy's voice, warning me. "Stay out of it, or you'll involve us all."

He watched us a moment, then turned and gave Amena a shove. Because she was blindfolded, she stumbled and almost fell. They took her down the hall and out of the building, holding her between them and pushing her along.

I didn't try to stop them. I didn't step forward and say, "Wait! You're making a mistake." My mouth felt dry, and my throat ached. I was aware of Chevy's hand on my arm. I wanted to tell the soldiers that Amena wasn't the way she looked—all scruffy and dirty. That there was a real person—a treasure—beneath the surface. But I didn't. I stood with the others and watched.

The *mudeera* went back to her office. The prison was silent. The seconds stretched into minutes. I went straight to my mat and began to pray for Amena. "Dear Father, don't let them

torture her. O God, comfort her!'' Waves of
cold chills came over me, and it seemed that
there was a dark, oppressive air over the whole
prison. Amena's death was certain, but not torture. ''O Lord, not torture!''

It seemed like a long time before we heard the
shots—a succession of sharp reports, breaking
the stillness. I began to tremble and couldn't
stop. I felt so cold—so cold, for I knew what had
happened to Amena, but I didn't know why it
had had to happen.

The soldiers stayed in the prison all night,
roaming the halls, stopping to look into the
rooms. ''Not to worry,'' the *mudeera* had said.
''You will be all right.'' I wondered if she had
told that to Amena, too.

I lay on my mat and closed my eyes and thought
of the little slippers Amena had made for
me . . . slippers to warm me against the long,
cold nights.

I must have fallen asleep just before morning.
When I opened my eyes, Anne handed me a cup
of coffee, and I saw that she was already dressed.
So was everybody else. They were dressed and
sitting on their mats, with their suitcases packed
beside them.

And I was still in my red nightgown. All my
belongings were in the room with me, and my
suitcase was still out on the table in the hall—on
the other side of the locked door.

I was sipping my coffee, wondering what to
do, when the key clicked in the lock and a soldier kicked open the door. *''Yalla! Yalla!''* he

ordered, and then he began a rapid string of Arabic instructions.

"OK," Mia translated. "This is it. Everybody out! We have twenty minutes. Then they're going to lock this place up again."

We had talked before about staying together when we were released, but everyone forgot. It was like a stampede. Chevy got as far as a bench outside our room, then sat down and burst into tears. When I went out to to get my suitcase, I saw her sitting there, wailing.

"Chevy!" I exclaimed. "What's the matter with you?" But she didn't answer me. She didn't seem able to talk at all. A soldier came by, picked up her suitcase, and she followed him out, still crying hysterically.

I grabbed my suitcase and lugged it into the room. Then I opened it and stood there in my nightgown trying to pack. My hands were shaking, just like that day long ago in customs, and I couldn't seem to think. What should I take? What should I leave? How was I going to get dressed in time to get out of here? I felt as if I were moving in slow motion. Everybody was running circles around me, and I couldn't seem to get myself going.

Suddenly, I realized that everybody was gone. I was in here alone, and I still wasn't ready to leave. I was hurriedly dressing when a man in civilian clothes came into the room and saw me there. He was about my age, rather short, and he hadn't shaved for days.

"*Yalla!*" he said. "Hurry up!" His accent was

293

heavy, but I could understand what he was saying.

"OK. OK. I'm hurrying as fast as I can."

But he didn't leave. He just stood there and looked at me. I stepped behind a cupboard that held some books so that he couldn't watch me as I finished dressing. I stepped into some black pants and put on a black blouse and a long, brown sweater. Then I came out where he could see me again and stood holding my red nightgown in my hand. I didn't want it, and I didn't know what to do with it. It seemed like such a big decision to make. Finally, I stuffed it into the suitcase and slammed the lid shut. I picked up my shoulder bag and my handbag and followed him out the door. He carried my suitcase for me, and we walked together down the hall.

The *mudeera* and Noha were standing on the other side of the screen, by the office, watching everybody leave. I went as close as I could to the *mudeera*. "Will I be taken to the American Embassy now? That's what you promised us last night."

She shrugged her shoulders. "I guess," she murmured.

I looked at the man carrying my suitcase, then at my shoulder bag, mentally checking myself out. Had I forgotten anything important? My coat! I had left my gray coat back in the room.

"Wait!" I cried. "Wait . . . just one minute!"

I turned and ran all the way back to the room and waited for one of the guards to unlock the door. I walked into the room and stopped. All the mats were there, just the way the girls had crawled out of them. Cups of still warm coffee sat cooling on empty boxes—those precious boxes that we had treasured so much. Food was lying on the open trough, and the cockroaches were already crawling over it. Everything was just as if we were still living there.

I picked up my coat and turned away. I never once looked back. At the front door, I waved to Noha, then walked down the pathway and out through the double gates I had entered almost two years before. The man in civilian clothes was still carrying my suitcase, walking a few steps ahead of me.

"Come, come, let's go this way," he said. We were on Sanayeh Street. It was deserted, desolate . . . everything had been evacuated. As we crossed the street, I saw Anne and Penny on the other side, standing beside a parked car.

"Marti," Anne called. "Come with us. We're going to the Carlton Hotel."

I started forward—hesitated. I wanted to be with them, yet something was holding me back. I felt a hand on my arm.

"No!" The man who was with me was insistent. "You not go with them. You stay with me." Then he lowered his voice. "Those are not good men. You stay with Joseph and hope nothing bad happens to those girls."

I didn't know whether to believe him or not. But the men Anne and Penny were with did look a little suspicious. I followed Joseph down the street toward a gas station that was surrounded by jeeps with tripod machine guns. The men all had red-and-white-checkered scarves around their heads and carried submachine guns in their arms.

We went into the station and Joseph put my suitcase by the window. There was a little table there with a phone on it. He motioned for me to sit down.

"You want coffee?" he asked.

"I want to go to the American Embassy."

He shook his head. "I can't take you there. Too dangerous for me."

"How about a taxi? I could call a taxi."

He grinned. "There are no taxis."

I was suddenly afraid. "Then I want to go back to Sanayeh—back to the prison." At least at the prison I would be alive, I thought. But Joseph shook his head.

Men in uniforms walked in and out of the station, pausing to look at me curiously. Joseph stood nearby, watching. Nobody was going to take me anywhere. I was the only woman there, and I was beginning to feel like that was the way they wanted it.

"Can I call the embassy?" I asked Joseph.

He grinned again and nodded.

I fumbled through my address book and found the number, then reached for the phone and started to dial. But there was no tone. The lines had been cut. There was no way to let the embassy know I was here. I put the phone down and looked at Joseph.

"You know," he said. "when we are finished

with people, they are usually just thankful for a cup of water."

What did he mean by that? Was he talking about me? I was too terrified to ask.

Suddenly he stood up. "We can't stay here any longer," he told me. "Must go now."

"Go where?"

"I take you to a friend's house. You can make phone call from there."

We got into one of the jeeps, rode a few blocks, and stopped in front of a large, two-story building surrounded by a big iron fence. We entered the ground-floor basement at the back of the house. The phone was on a bookcase with Palestinian posters above it on the walls. I picked up the receiver and dialed the embassy number. The phone rang, but no one answered.

"It's only six-thrity in the morning," Joseph said. "That is too early for anyone to be in the office."

I looked around for a place to sit. There was a bed along one wall, and I sat gingerly on its edge. I could feel my knees trembling. I didn't want to be in this place. Why hadn't I just walked back to the prison when I was still within walking distance?

Joseph stood in front of me, watching me, always watching. "Are you afraid?" he asked.

"No. Why should I be afraid?"

He sat down on the bed next to me. "You don't need to be afraid."

I didn't like the tone of his voice. It was too smooth, too suggestive. "I think I'll try the embassy again," I said. My fingers were trembling as I dialed. The phone rang, then rang again. There was a click at the other end.

"Hello . . . hello. . . ." It was a man's voice, speaking English with an American accent.

"Oh, thank God!" I exclaimed. "My name is Marti Sinclair, and I want to come to the embassy. I need to have a passport to get out of the country."

"Yes, ma'am," he said in a matter-of-fact voice. "This is the security guard. The consul isn't here yet, but if you'll just give me your address and phone number. . . ."

"No, no, you don't understand. I'm Marti Sinclair. I just got out of Sanayeh. Please come and get me. I'm afraid."

I could see Joseph out of the corner of my eye. He was smiling. "I thought you were afraid," he said.

"Where are you?" asked the voice on the phone.

"I don't know. Somewhere not too far from the prison."

I heard him groan. "Well, give me your phone number then."

"I don't know that, either. There isn't any number on the phone."

Joseph was standing next to me. "Do you want me to tell them?" he asked. I nodded, and he took the receiver and spoke into it, giving directions. I had no way of telling if they were right or wrong, because I didn't know where I was. He handed the receiver back to me, but he didn't move away.

"OK," came the voice on the other end. "As soon as it's safe enough on the streets, we'll try to come and get you."

When would that be? Thirty minutes? Four hours? Tomorrow? Never? I sat back down on the bed to wait.

"A woman was shot last night," Joseph told me. I didn't answer, and he came over and stood in front of me. "She was a spy."

Oh, no! Did they think I was a spy, too? Had Joseph given the wrong directions to the guard at the embassy? Were they going to blindfold me and take me outside and shoot me as they had shot Amena? The door burst open, and a man in civilian clothes wearing dark glasses and holding a machine gun walked in. He stared at me a minute, then began speaking Arabic to Joseph. I was terrified of him. I was sure he had come to take me away and kill me. "Father, help me. Don't let me panic. Please, dear Lord, be with me now and give me your strength!"

It seemed as if they talked a long time, looking at each other and then at me, as if they were trying to make up their minds. Their voices rose in argument. Then Joseph shrugged, and the other man came slowly toward me.

"Do you want some food?" he asked.

I tried to breathe slowly—to make my heart stop beating so fast. "I—I could drink a cup of coffee."

Joseph brought it, and I sipped it slowly, holding the cup with both hands so they wouldn't see how hard I was shaking. Joseph sat beside me on the bed. "You don't be afraid," he said.

"We don't hurt you." He reached out his hand and put it on my knee.

"Oh, God, please help me. I don't know what to do."

There was a loud buzzing in my ears, and a wave of nausea passed through me, leaving me weak and trembling. I closed my eyes. For the first time in my life, I hoped that I would faint. Vaguely, I heard the door open and close—the sound of a man's voice. Now there were three of them, I thought. I didn't have a chance.

CHAPTER

25

"Marti . . . Marti Sinclair? I'm the vice-consul from the American Embassy."

I opened my eyes and stared at the American who extended his hand to me. His grasp was warm and firm as he helped me to my feet. "You are the most beautiful sight I have ever seen," I told him.

A few moments later, I was in the embassy car, answering questions. "Marti, I want you to tell me everything you can remember," he said. "Start with yesterday, and tell me who came to the prison. What did they look like? What did they do? Do you have any idea who those men were that you were with just now?"

I told him all I could and then I asked him about the other girls. But he didn't have much to tell me. Chevy was at Esther's house, but none of the others had been found. They had reason to believe that Anne and Penny had been kidnapped. The British Embassy had already issued a bulletin demanding their immediate return. And the American Embassy had sent out a communiqué about Suzanne, trying to see if she could be located in any of the Palestinian camps.

I felt such heartache for them. I was safe now, but they were still out there somewhere. Tears ran down my cheeks as I began to pray for their safety. "Father, please . . . please be with them. Give them your strength as you gave it to me. Protect them, Lord. Please be with them in their time of need."

We went into the consul's office at the embassy, and I went out and stood for a second on the balcony where I could look over Beirut. Anne and Penny kidnapped . . . Suzanne missing. . . .

I could see the blue Mediterranean and the bombed-out, empty shells that had once been the Phoenicia Hotel and the Holiday Inn. There were men with machine guns stationed on all the roofs and in front of the embassy grounds. The other girls could be anywhere out there—lost and frightened—and in danger.

"Come back in here!" the consul ordered. "You're not safe standing on the balcony like that. We never know when they'll start firing again. We've even had to issue helmets to the embassy staff."

The phone rang, and it was Esther, telling them to bring me to her house for the night. It rang again, and it was Mary Mathias, calling from the mountains to see if I was all right.

The consul was processing my papers and getting a passport ready, and he had money for me from my father. "I'm putting you in a car," he said. "The driver will take you to a travel office where you can book an early flight out tomorrow."

I sat alone in the backseat and looked out at the rubble-filled streets. There were no sounds except for an occasional shout, a burst of gunfire, and the steady low roar of the car's engine. No horns honking or people laughing. No women calling to each other from their windows. The venders with their fruit carts were gone, replaced by young boys holding machine guns. I leaned farther back against the seat, glad I was riding safely in the embassy car.

We slowed down and turned into a narrow side street. Just ahead on my left I saw a figure hunched in the doorway of a small neighborhood grocery store. It was the figure of a woman, dressed in clothes that I had seen before. A thin woman with long black hair.

It was Suzanne! She looked frightened and lost, and there was no doubt that she was in danger. "Stop!" I yelled. Then I reached over and touched the driver on the shoulder. "Please stop the car and back up. There's a girl back there at the entrance of the little store. I know her. She's an American, and she's lost. We have to help her."

He put the car in reverse and backed up. When he came to the store, he stopped and honked his horn. I saw Suzanne look up, startled.

I opened the car door and got out. "Suzanne!" I yelled. "Suzanne!"

"Get back in this car!" the driver ordered. But I couldn't. I ran across the street and grabbed her by the arm.

"Come on, Suzanne! This is the embassy car."

Her face was white with fear. She stared at me as if I were a stranger. Then her features crumpled, and she began to cry. Great sobs shook her shoulders. I could feel her trembling all over. "Marti . . ." she said. "Oh, Marti, I—I thought I was dead."

I put my arms around her. "I know," I told her. "I know just how you feel."

"I'm—I'm so glad to see you, Marti." I hesitated. What could I say?

Whatever you feel like saying, Marti.

I took a deep breath and let it out slowly. "Well, Suzanne," I told her. "Believe it or not, I'm glad to see you, too."

We lifted her suitcase together, and carried it between us across the street. The driver got out and heaved it into the back of the car. We sat in the backseat. Just the two of us. Suzanne reached over once and touched me on the arm.

Almost without thinking, I put my hand over her hand. "We're going home, Suzanne," I told her. "We're really going home."

Esther fixed dinner for us that night—for Chevy and Suzanne and me. We sat at a real table, in real chairs, and ate with silver and china instead of plastic. But it was a subdued meal, for Anne and Penny had still not been found.

Later, while I was doing the dishes, I stood at the sink for a long time, praying, and letting the warm water run over my hands. Before I went to sleep, I asked Chevy if she had remembered to turn off the hot plate in our room at the prison. She looked at me and began to laugh. "I turned it off, Marti, but what does it matter now?"

In the morning, before it was even light, the embassy car was waiting for Suzanne and me, and our good-byes were brief. The consul was anxious to get us on the airplane that morning, because there were problems about our departure. Officially, we had never been released. We had escaped from prison and were fugitives-at-large. There was a chance we could be re-arrested and taken to another prison. Special arrangements were still being made to try to get us out of the country as quickly as possible.

Suzanne and I were waiting nervously in an office at the airport when Penny and Anne walked in. There were dark circles beneath their eyes, and their lids looked swollen, as if they had been crying. They seemed so tired, and both of them moved slowly, as if each step were painful.

"What happened?" I asked. "We've all been worried sick. Are you both all right?"

Anne's voice was soft, almost a whisper. "We spent the night in protective custody," she said. "When we left Sanayeh, those men waiting outside told us we couldn't go to the British Embassy. That's why we told you we were going to the Carlton Hotel . . . to the Australian Embassy. We were sure they would help us.

"The soldiers offered to drive us there, but they went in the wrong direction. We were afraid to get out and walk, because they said we would be shot without proper IDs. They took us to an apartment. There were five of them, Marti, and—and they all had guns.''

Her voice broke, and she covered her face with her hands. ''They told us they had had no women for two months, and if we didn't cooperate, they would kill us. Then they began to hit us, just to show they meant it.

''We were so scared, Marti. We were too scared to fight. They took turns with us all day. They. . . .'' Tears were streaming down her face. Penny had leaned against the wall and closed her eyes.

There was nothing I could do but stand there with them and listen and feel their pain and tell them that I had been praying for them the whole time they were missing.

''They let us go,'' Anne said, ''because they heard the British Embassy was looking for us.'' Her lips quivered, but she tried to smile. ''Marti, listen. While it . . . while it was happening, I prayed to your God—the one I said I didn't believe in—and I said that if he were really there—that if he would just save our lives—I would believe in him. Oh, Marti, we really are alive. It's all over now, isn't it? We're really going home, aren't we, Marti?''

The office door opened, and the American and British Embassy representatives came in. We watched their faces anxiously. They couldn't send us back to prison. They just couldn't. Not now.

But they were smiling. ''You can relax,'' the American said. ''It was touch and go for a while, but everything is OK. I want all of you to get airborne before they can change their minds!''

We walked out of the airport together and climbed the steps to our plane. A cool breeze was blowing, and the night sky was fading into dawn. I sat in my seat and buckled my seat belt. I heard the engines roar. The plane began to move—slowly, slowly down the runway. I put my face close to the window and looked out, watching the darkness break and the early morning light slip through.

I remembered . . . oh, the things I remembered. But we were going home. We were alive, and we were going home. It had been a long, dark night into morning. I had seen the winter of my soul. But now the sun was rising. Sunrise over Sanayeh. It was the beginning of a new day.

You will forget your misery;
  you will remember it as waters
    that have passed away.
And your life will be brighter
  than the noonday;
    its darkness will be like the morning.
And you will have confidence,
  because there is hope;
    you will be protected and take
      your rest in safety.
                                        —Job 11:16–18, RSV

EPILOGUE

Today, Marti Sinclair lives in San Francisco, California, and works at her church as a staff member.

Her return to society after twenty-one months in prison was not an easy transition. When she came home, Marti was not the same person she had been. Her old personality had been stripped away, and, though joyous at being free, she wondered what it was that God expected her to do with the new life he had given her.

Searching for the ministry God had for her, Marti went to Oregon to see Bob and Jessie Paeth and to look for work. The job she had thought God wanted for her as director of a residential treatment home for women fell through, and she returned home in the summer of 1976 feeling temporarily despondent and discouraged.

But it was not long before she felt God's plan for her begin to unfold. On a Wednesday morning in September she met with the Women's Growth Ministry—a small group of church women who came together to share their thoughts, to pray, to grow. This, Marti says, was the key to her new life.

Then, at God's appointed time, she was hired as executive secretary at a Christian high school, where she worked for five years.

Her lifeline, Marti says, is in the heartbeat of the church. Today, she is still active in the Women's Growth Ministry, where she shares the leadership of a small group. Working in a team from the church, she has done counseling as well as two prayer seminars for women and two retreats for college youth.

Looking back over the years of her new life, Marti says, "It has been like a journey in prayers answered and in seeing God work in exciting ways. The things about me that I never thought could be changed—have been changed. God is there, and he is not silent. He does hear and answer prayers. He is miraculous. He brought me out of myself and let me reach out to others."

Other Living Books Bestsellers

THE BEST CHRISTMAS PAGEANT EVER by Barbara Robinson. A delightfully wild and funny story about what can happen to a Christmas program when the "horrible Herdman" family of brothers and sisters are miscast in the roles of the Christmas story characters from the Bible. 07-0137 $2.50.

ELIJAH by William H. Stephens. He was a rough-hewn farmer who strolled onto the stage of history to deliver warnings to Ahab the king and to defy Jezebel the queen. A powerful biblical novel you will never forget. 07-4023 $3.50.

THE TOTAL MAN by Dan Benson. A practical guide on how to gain confidence and fulfillment. Covering areas such as budgeting of time, money matters, and marital relationships. 07-7289 $3.50.

HOW TO HAVE ALL THE TIME YOU NEED EVERY DAY by Pat King. Drawing from her own and other women's experiences as well as from the Bible and the research of time experts, Pat has written a warm and personal book for every Christian woman. 07-1529 $2.95.

IT'S INCREDIBLE by Ann Kiemel. "It's incredible" is what some people say when a slim young woman says, "Hi. I'm Ann," and starts talking about love and good and beauty. As Ann tells about a Jesus who can make all the difference in their lives, some call that incredible, and turn away. Others become miracles themselves, agreeing with Ann that it's incredible. 07-1818 $2.50.

EVERGREEN CASTLES by Laurie Clifford. A heartwarming story about the growing pains of five children whose hilarious adventures teach them unforgettable lessons about love and forgiveness, life and death. Delightful reading for all ages. 07-0779 $2.95.

JOHN, SON OF THUNDER by Ellen Gunderson Traylor. Travel with John down the desert paths, through the courts of the Holy City, and to the foot of the cross. Journey with him from his luxury as a privileged son of Israel to the bitter hardship of his exile on Patmos. This is a saga of adventure, romance, and discovery—of a man bigger than life—the disciple "whom Jesus loved." 07-1903 $3.95.

WHAT'S IN A NAME? compiled by Linda Francis, John Hartzel, and Al Palmquist. A fascinating name dictionary that features the literal meaning of people's first names, the character quality implied by the name, and an applicable Scripture verse for each name listed. Ideal for expectant parents! 07-7935 $2.95.

Other Living Books Bestsellers

DAVID AND BATHSHEBA by Roberta Kells Dorr. Was Bathsheba an innocent country girl or a scheming adulteress? What was King David really like? Solomon—the wisest man in the world—was to be king, but could he survive his brothers' intrigues? Here is an epic love story which comes radiantly alive through the art of a fine storyteller. 07-0618 $3.95.

TOO MEAN TO DIE by Nick Pirovolos with William Proctor. In this action-packed story, Nick the Greek tells how he grew from a scrappy immigrant boy to a fearless underworld criminal. Finally caught, he was imprisoned. But something remarkable happened and he was set free—truly set free! 07-7283 $3.50.

FOR WOMEN ONLY. This bestseller gives a balanced, entertaining, diversified treatment of all aspects of womanhood. Edited by Evelyn and J. Allan Petersen, founder of Family Concern. 07-0897 $3.50.

FOR MEN ONLY. Edited by J. Allan Petersen, this book gives solid advice on how men can cope with the tremendous pressures they face every day as fathers, husbands, workers. 07-0892 $3.50.

ROCK. What is rock music really doing to you? Bob Larson presents a well-researched and penetrating look at today's rock music and rock performers. What are lyrics really saying? Who are the top performers and what are their life-styles? 07-5686 $2.95.

THE ALCOHOL TRAP by Fred Foster. A successful film executive was about to lose everything—his family's vacation home, his house in New Jersey, his reputation in the film industry, his wife. This is an emotion-packed story of hope and encouragement, offering valuable insights into the troubled world of high pressure living and alcoholism. 07-0078 $2.95.

LET ME BE A WOMAN. Best selling author Elisabeth Elliot (author of *THROUGH GATES OF SPLENDOR*) presents her profound and unique perspective on womanhood. This is a significant book on a continuing controversial subject. 07-2162 $2.95.

WE'RE IN THE ARMY NOW by Imeldia Morris Eller. Five children become their older brother's "army" as they work together to keep their family intact during a time of crisis for their mother. 07-7862 $2.95.

WILD CHILD by Mari Hanes. A heartrending story of a young boy who was abandoned and struggled alone for survival. You will be moved as you read how one woman's love tamed this boy who was more animal than human. 07-0223 $2.95.

THE SURGEON'S FAMILY by David Hernandez with Carole Gift Page. This is an incredible three-generation story of a family that has faced danger and death—and has survived. Walking dead-end streets of violence and poverty, often seemingly without hope, the family of David Hernandez has struggled to find a new kind of life. 07-6684 $2.95.

Other Living Books Bestsellers

THE MAN WHO COULD DO NO WRONG by Charles E. Blair with John and Elizabeth Sherrill. He built one of the largest churches in America . . . then he made a mistake. This is the incredible story of Pastor Charles E. Blair, accused of massive fraud. A book "for error-prone people in search of the Christian's secret for handling mistakes." 07-4002 $3.50.

GIVERS, TAKERS AND OTHER KINDS OF LOVERS by Josh McDowell. This book bypasses vague generalities about love and sex and gets right down to basic questions: Whatever happened to sexual freedom? What's true love like? What is your most important sex organ? Do men respond differently than women? If you're looking for straight answers about God's plan for love and sexuality then this book was written for you. 07-1023 $2.50.

MORE THAN A CARPENTER by Josh McDowell. This best selling author thought Christians must be "out of their minds." He put them down. He argued against their faith. But eventually he saw that his arguments wouldn't stand up. In this book, Josh focuses upon the person who changed his life—Jesus Christ. 07-4552 $2.50.

HIND'S FEET ON HIGH PLACES by Hannah Hurnard. A classic allegory which has sold more than a million copies! 07-1429 $3.50.

THE CATCH ME KILLER by Bob Erler with John Souter. Golden gloves, black belt, green beret, silver badge. Supercop Bob Erler had earned the colors of manhood. Now can he survive prison life? An incredible true story of forgiveness and hope. 07-0214 $3.50.

WHAT WIVES WISH THEIR HUSBANDS KNEW ABOUT WOMEN by Dr. James Dobson. By the best selling author of *DARE TO DISCIPLINE* and *THE STRONG-WILLED CHILD*, here's a vital book that speaks to the unique emotional needs and aspirations of today's woman. An immensely practical, interesting guide. 07-7896 $2.95.

PONTIUS PILATE by Dr. Paul Maier. This fascinating novel is about one of the most famous Romans in history—the man who declared Jesus innocent but who nevertheless sent him to the cross. This powerful biblical novel gives you a unique insight into the life and death of Jesus. 07-4852 $3.50.

BROTHER OF THE BRIDE by Donita Dyer. This exciting sequel to *THE BRIDE'S ESCAPE* tells of the faith of a proud, intelligent Armenian family whose Christian heritage stretched back for centuries. A story of suffering, separation, valor, victory, and reunion. 07-0179 $2.95.

LIFE IS TREMENDOUS by Charlie Jones. Believing that enthusiasm makes the difference, Jones shows how anyone can be happy, involved, relevant, productive, healthy, and secure in the midst of a high-pressure, commercialized, automated society. 07-2184 $2.50.

HOW TO BE HAPPY THOUGH MARRIED by Dr. Tim LaHaye. One of America's most successful marriage counselors gives practical, proven advice for marital happiness. 07-1499 $2.95.

The books listed are available at your bookstore. If unavailable, send check with order to cover retail price plus 10% for postage and handling to:

Tyndale House Publishers, Inc.
Box 80
Wheaton, Illinois 60189

Prices and availability subject to change without notice. Allow 4-6 weeks for delivery.